This is the best book on self-sabotage that I have put my hands on. Trinity Jordan has captured the essence of man's mortal enemy and marks for us the sure way to victory. I highly recommend this book for believers everywhere. Your life will not be the same after reading and applying this one-of-a-kind message.

—RICH WILKERSON
FOUNDER, PEACEMAKERS
SENIOR PASTOR, TRINITY CHURCH

Trinity Jordan has done a masterful job of uncovering the one thing that keeps us away from living the life God has for us to live—insecurity. In his book *Sabotage* readers will have a good look in the mirror. While they may not like what they see at first, as they undertake this journey, they will come to see themselves in the light of God's amazing love and grace. Trinity is up-front, hilarious, and transparent as he reveals his firsthand experiences and lessons learned from his own battles with insecurity.

—MIKE FOSTER
PEOPLE OF THE SECOND CHANCE

Blessed is the leader who knows how to manage their own insecurities, while influencing others who are held hostage by theirs! *Sabotage* is a great reminder that "we are God's masterpiece" and is a must-read for the leader who is serious about accomplishing the good deeds that He has prepared for us to do.

—Doug Clay
General Treasurer, Assemblies of God
Author, *Dreaming in 3D*

In *Sabotage* Trinity Jordan unmasks an often-overlooked enemy disrupting the lives of too many Christians. This may be the first and only book on "insecurity management," and it's a good one. With a style that is both entertaining and insightful, Trinity uses powerful examples from the life of Jacob the patriarch woven together with transparent stories from his own journey to reveal the perils of insecurity and how to keep it from destroying you. It's a helpful book for every follower of Christ but a must-read for church leaders!

—Steve Pike
National Director, Church
Multiplication Network

Insecurity will kill you. And Trinity gives a brilliant way to avoid it. Leaders need to deal with this more than anyone. And this book will illuminate many of the pitfalls. Trinity is funny, honest, and insightful. *Sabotage* is a perfect read for anyone who wants to lead with freedom, generosity, and genuine love.

—PETER HAAS
PASTOR, SUBSTANCE CHURCH, MINNEAPOLIS, MINNESOTA
AUTHOR, *PHARISECTOMY: HOW TO JOYFULLY REMOVE YOUR INNER PHARISEE AND OTHER RELIGIOUSLY TRANSMITTED DISEASES*

In these pages Trinity's vulnerability challenges the reader to face their own personal insecurities now so they avoid a train wreck later. If you read this book, you will grow emotionally, psychologically, and spiritually.

—BRYAN JARRETT
LEAD PASTOR, NORTHPLACE CHURCH
AUTHOR, *EXTRAVAGANT*

Trinity Jordan states truths that I believe would have been eye-opening in my battle to trust God for wholeness. My life was plagued during my reliance on food, but this journey through obesity, the journey of finding a new place of health spiritually as well as emotionally and physically has been completely founded in learning to quit sabotaging me. I can see myself rereading Jordan's words to remind me of who I trust so I do not sabotage my life again.

—AUSTIN ANDREWS
CONTESTANT ON *THE BIGGEST LOSER*
RETROFIT MINISTRIES

SABOTAGE

TRINITY JORDAN

PASSIO

Most CHARISMA HOUSE BOOK GROUP products are available at special quantity discounts for bulk purchase for sales promotions, premiums, fund-raising, and educational needs. For details, write Charisma House Book Group, 600 Rinehart Road, Lake Mary, Florida 32746, or telephone (407) 333-0600.

SABOTAGE by Trinity Jordan
Published by Passio
Charisma Media/Charisma House Book Group
600 Rinehart Road
Lake Mary, Florida 32746
www.charismahouse.com

Unless otherwise noted, all Scripture quotations are from are from the Holy Bible, English Standard Version. Copyright © 2001 by Crossway Bibles, a division of Good News Publishers. Used by permission.

Scripture quotations marked THE MESSAGE are from *The Message: The Bible in Contemporary English*, copyright © 1993, 1994, 1995, 1996, 2000, 2001, 2002. Used by permission of NavPress Publishing Group.

Cover design by Justin Evans
Design Director: Bill Johnson

Visit the author's website at trinityjordan.org.

Library of Congress Control Number: 2012956141
International Standard Book Number: 978-1-62136-048-3
E-book ISBN: 978-1-62136-049-0

While the author has made every effort to provide accurate
telephone numbers and Internet addresses at the time of
publication, neither the publisher nor the author assumes
any responsibility for errors or for changes that occur after
publication.

First edition

13 14 15 16 17 — 9 8 7 6 5 4 3 2 1
Printed in the United States of America

.

To my wife, Ami.
You are my best friend and make me feel so
wanted.
(I love you more. There it is in print—I win.)

To my daughter Madison.
Your giggles brighten even the darkest days.

To my daughter Berlyn.
Your tenderness makes me feel special.

This book is for all of you.

CONTENTS

FOREWORD

TRINITY JORDAN HAS fully exposed one of the main tactics the enemy uses to steal abundant life from us—insecurity. I found myself laughing and cringing at the same time as I read this book. And I could definitely relate to the hilariously embarrassing and highly impactful personal stories that my friend shares.

I love Trinity's authenticity. He bares all and leaves nothing to the imagination. He puts himself on the line in this book to set readers free from their own insecurities. His simple and unassuming approach is refreshing. And I challenge you to not just read this book but to also take a long look in the mirror.

We need to come face-to-face with ourselves and our desire to maintain a sense of security by any desperate means possible. This drive and pursuit of securing "a life" for ourselves is the main thing that causes us to take matters out of God's hands and attempt to build monuments for ourselves. In turn we sabotage and cheat ourselves out of living the amazing life Christ died to give us. Trinity points out that it is simply a lack of trust—a disbelief that God can handle our lives and bring about the best outcome possible. At the soul level, our insecurity proves that we do not trust in His infinite, eternal perspective. Yet somehow we trust our own limited and small perspective to dictate our future and what we should and should not have. It's truly inconceivable, really, how we place a greater trust in our vision over God's.

Trinity's stories are my stories. And as you dive into this life-changing book, you will see that his stories are your stories too. He effectively has hit the nail on the head when it comes to diagnosing the sad human condition outside a surrendered life in Christ.

Sabotage (this book) coerces you into a place of honesty from which real and deep healing comes. In this place paradigms shift and perspectives change. You will learn that true control comes from letting go and letting God. And that true authority comes from humility. Trinity says that the root of insecurity is a focus on ourselves—what hand we were dealt in life, why weren't we picked for that special assignment, why did God allow this to happen to us. It's all about us.

Insecurity sabotages our ability to love God, love people, and love ourselves, which is the true essence of our whole purpose for being created. If you hold on to insecurity, you will end up living a life you were not meant to live, and you still will not find any contentment, joy, or fulfillment. You will always be reaching for the next mirage that won't bring you the security that only God can.

You may not have had the best parents, the best education, lived in the best neighborhood, or any other thing that fell short. Trinity says, "We don't get to pick the ingredients for our lives. God does. But here's the thing. The right ingredients, blended together, make the best recipes possible." How true.

If we can trust God with the recipe and the blending, if we can say, "Yes, Lord," and stay out of His way, then there is nothing God cannot do in us and through us. We will find perfect security in Him.

God will not let you down. He will not leave you or forsake you. I believe that God has given you a vision of greatness, and He will provide for it as you trust Him and submit your plans humbly to Him. You can take back enemy territory in your life by allowing God to move you from insecurity to security in Him.

God gives grace to the humble. Grace is the supernatural ability to perform God-sized feats that will radically change your world and the world around you. God will accomplish great things through us when we let go of insecurity.

Let God amaze you with His grace and favor as you take this courageous journey with Trinity Jordan.

Stay humble. Stay hungry.

—Mark Batterson
Lead Pastor, National Community Church,
Washington DC
New York Times Best-Selling Author, *The Circle Maker*

ACKNOWLEDGMENTS

EVERYTHING I LEARNED, I learned from someone else. I can take no credit for anything in this book. I am just the medium to provide the information now in your hands.

Debbie Marrie and Jevon Bolden, it was a pleasure working with you on this project. Thank you for believing in me and allowing me to write the book I always wanted to write.

Ryan Lind, not only do I look up to you, but I have always felt you were an older brother who has guided me with wisdom, intelligence, and wit. Your edits to this manuscript were not just a help in making this a better book, but they were also miniature teaching sessions for my life and writing ability as an author. You motivated me, and I will forever be grateful for our friendship in my life. Remember me when you are a rock star.

And thanks to my wife, Ami. Thank you for being so patient with me. All the countless hours I spent reading and writing, moving our family all over the country, traveling from place to place—you dealt with all of it with a smile on your face. You are the best gift God has ever placed in my life. I am complete with you. This book wouldn't be possible without you.

INTRODUCTION

EVERYONE WHO HAS ever been to law school remembers the first day of classes. I am like the majority and remember mine all too well. My incoming class was more than four hundred people from every walk of life, and we gathered on that first day for our orientation to what would be our law school experience.

I really had no clue what to expect on that first day. We had been e-mailed reading assignments for mock classes, and the reading assignments you received depended on your last name.

It didn't take much of a leap in logic to understand that prepping the reading assignments for the mock classes on orientation day had more to do with setting a good example for whatever professor oversaw your mock class than for receiving an actual grade. I read my assigned reading, read the hypothetical case, and concluded that the once-over I'd given the reading was good enough for what I was supposed to get out of the mock class.

It felt like junior high all over again, as my classmates and I were cattle-driven to our assigned classrooms for the day and socially awkward at best in our attempts to make new friends. The only difference was that we were all dressed in business attire instead of jeans and T-shirts.

As I sat down in an empty row, another student who started to quiz me on the case we'd been assigned joined me. I then realized I had read the wrong case (apparently not knowing how to look up my last name properly).

I shrugged it off, though. Again, I felt I understood the expectation for orientation day and how it fit into the bigger scheme of the new law school experience.

Some of my classmates had other expectations.

Sitting in the front row of each mock class I had that day was the oldest student in our class—a second-career student in his mid-forties, a 1992 Dell laptop opened on the desk in front of him, complete with color-coded notes on the screen, himself attentive and ready. Every word that flowed from the mouth of each professor that day was meticulously recorded by this student on his trusty Dell laptop (which seemed to have the nosiest key compression sound in the world).

This student had expectations that went far beyond those of anyone else in the room.

For instance, in these mock classes a professor would ask a series of questions and volunteers would offer their answers. But as each volunteer began to dialogue with the professor, this older student would interrupt halfway through the volunteer's explanations to inject his own thoughts into the conversation. These continuous interruptions became almost comical by the end of the day, with the rest of us anticipating his fervent behavior more and more.

Clearly this student's expectation was not to make a poor, perhaps hostile impression on his fellow classmates and professors that day. His expectation was not to receive information about the school and course load or to prepare for the upcoming experience of law school based on the day's proceedings.

Instead, he assumed he was supposed to prove to the rest of us and our professors that he knew more than anyone else and that law school was something he would conquer.

In the same way, coming into this book, you could have one of two expectations. One would be the expectation of dialogue, of being open to a give and take about the subject we're going to explore together. The other would be the expectation to prove me and everything written in this book wrong.

My friend Steve Pike said to me one time that insecurity was the "silent killer" of a person's life. That statement drips with truth. Insecurity lives deep inside of each of us, and it slowly corrodes the fabric of our self-image, our relationship with one another, and our relationship with God. It sabotages relationships that should be, could be, and would be. Your expectation should be to find a glimpse into the sabotaging disease that exists in our lives and learn to identify what might already exist.

If your expectation in reading this book is to prove what I say is wrong, then you might want to stop reading right now. If your expectation is to walk away from reading this book with no more insecurities, then you might want to stop reading right now too.

I am not Freud, nor do I possess adequate training to diagnose or dissect complex psychological issues. All I have is a human understanding of the pages of what those of us who follow Jesus call sacred Scriptures.

And I believe I am 51 percent right in my understanding.

This book is an attempt to articulate that understanding in a way that might help us both live out of the freedom God intends to give us. My attempt is not perfect, nor do I proclaim that it is, but I hope it will effectuate a response from the depths to question, answer, change, respond, or bow to God's supreme sovereignty in our lives.

Hopefully in that process we will let go of the areas that drive us to insecurity and sabotage our lives. Hopefully we can walk away convicted, aware, and alert to the already existing insecurities in our lives. *Insecurity* is usually a term reserved for the wallflower stranger who doesn't make eye contact in a social situation, but insecurity is the dormant disease that lives in all of us. It manifests itself in a bunch of different ways in each one of our lives, but what is always true is that each manifestation sabotages the life God wants for us.

That being said, I'll warn you right now that you may find yourself wanting to throw this book across the room as you read the somewhat bleak walk we take through human nature in these pages. You may feel at times that the story is oversimplified or there is no hope.

Wait it out.

I studied, pored over notes of everything I heard taught on this subject, and pressed hard into the pages of the Bible for a glimpse at the reality of insecurity in our lives and the reality of hope.

At times I too wanted to chuck the Macbook on which I was writing these words clear across the room. But it was in this wrestling, in this struggle, that I felt something might be accomplished in the search for understanding and resolution to our insecurities.

I don't believe this book is the final word on insecurity.

I do, however, believe it is a start.

Well, maybe saying it's a start isn't really correct either. Many others have come before me to articulate their understanding and thoughts on this same subject.

Maybe the best way for me to explain this book, then, is to say that it's a separate dialogue in the continuation of a discussion that has existed since the beginning of the fall of man. It is *one* of the pieces, but it is not the *final* piece.

And yet.

As followers of Christ, we might find there is more power in dialogue than we realize when we first walk into the conversation. Dialogue forces us to interact with the material, making it something we must integrate in our thinking and understanding, and not just something we can passively glaze over. Dialogue forces us to respond. Dialogue requires an exchange. And it is in this forced interaction, response, and exchange that our lives actually change. Knowledge in and of itself doesn't change us, but the use of knowledge processed into the depths of our being moves us to belief, which moves us to action, which moves us to change.

I believe with all that is inside me that if we trust God with every fiber of who we are as we attempt this pursuit together, then by the work of the Spirit inside of us we will see the sabotage negated in the end.

That is my hope.

That is the expectation I have for this book.

That is what you should expect.

Part I

SUBVERSION

.

Chapter 1

THE SABOTAGE BEGINS

No man really knows about other
human beings. The best he can do is
to suppose that they are like himself.[1]
—JOHN STEINBECK

J AKE CAME FROM a great family by everybody's standards.

Wealthy.

Well-known.

Respected.

He had it all.

Think of Jake's family as the Kennedys—lineage you would be proud to call your own.

Jake's grandfather was the patriarch of his religious community. It was said that Jake's grandfather spoke with God. He had received specific instructions from God: "This is how you should live. This is how you will become prosperous on the earth. If you do these things, then your name will not pass away, your progeny and their renown will be great, and you will bless the world."

Now this was a promise, a possible outcome. An "if you follow Me…then I" agreement. Grandpa was considered a man of faith, a man of God, and his family represented a lifeline, a hope by which God would connect with the rest of the world.

Jake's grandfather would later become enshrined in antiquity for his faith in God and how he lived his life in light of God.

Maybe you have a grandparent known for his or her faith, for his time spent in the family Bible—the Bible that has been handed down to the next generation—or for her seemingly supernatural ability to pray, sometimes for hours, with uncanny results.

Jake's grandfather was their template.

On top of all that Jake's dad was somewhat of a miracle to his grandfather's blessings from God. He was the firstborn to an aging couple who had lost all hope of having children of their own. Now Jake's dad had fulfilled all their hopes and dreams. He would continue on the life of Jake's grandfather and the family blessing.

Dad struggled to set himself apart from Grandpa, though. Grandpa cast such a big shadow that it was hard for Dad to really be his own man and put his own stamp on life. Plus, Grandma was a little overprotective of her miracle baby—and why wouldn't she be? This was everything she had hoped for: a son of her own. And as men do, usually marrying someone like their mothers, Dad did just that. He married a wonderful woman who, in turn, became very controlling of her husband and Jake.

This promise from God, this blessing that had moved from Grandpa to Dad would now move through Jake and his siblings to the rest of the world, would continue its movement through this great family tree.

Only one problem for Jake, though.

He wasn't the firstborn.

He wasn't the patriarch who heard from God.

He wasn't even the miracle baby of the patriarch.

He was simply the younger brother.

You see, in Jake's culture the firstborn son was the one who would take on the mantle of the family lineage, wealth, power, and fame.

That wasn't Jake, though.

He was the second-born—a twin, sure, but nonetheless born too late.

He was the second son.

And no one strives for second. No one wants second place.

Second means you're not at the top. You're not the winner.

Second means you don't get what first gets.

Second means you get lost in the story of history.

Who was Abraham Lincoln's younger brother?

Who lost to Usain Bolt in the one-hundred-meter dash?

Who graduated number two in your class? Number one gave that rambling, nervous speech on graduation day. Who didn't ramble?

That was Jake.

Second.

Jake never was content with second. In fact, the story goes that even at birth, Jake was holding on to his brother's heel, almost as if trying to stop him from going first out the birth canal. His parents named him Jacob, after this birth event, because in his native tongue *Jacob* means, "he takes by the heel."

Jake's older brother, Esau, on the other hand, was what you would describe as a man's man. He probably barked like Tim Allen and wore plaid shirts like the Brawny man.

He was a hunter by skill and trade.

A man of the outdoors.

Aggressive.

Intimidating.

Fierce.

And extremely hairy.

He was the picture-perfect son to take on the reins of this great family. He was a mighty man who could conquer, who could instill awe in those around him, and who by physical appearance could command others to follow him. If you were going to pass off your promises from God to someone, Esau's shoulders could handle the load.

People would later write that Esau was Dad's favorite boy. By the physical looks of things, it was easy to see why people would say this.

Esau.

The firstborn.

Son of Isaac, the miracle baby.

Grandson of Abraham, the patriarch of Judaism.

Twin older brother of Jacob.

Not second, but first.

And extremely hairy.

Esau and Jacob's birth story would not be the last time Jacob would try to be first in the family. Jake wasn't content being second. Something inside of him longed for freedom from the pain of being second, and he was willing to do anything to medicate the pain.

Anything.

Even if it cost him his identity.

Not Just a Story in the Bible

Jake's story is really our story.

If we're honest with ourselves, we can look around and admit we're not happy with who we are, what we've done with our time on earth, and what we have been given.

Younger sibling.

Poor family.

Rich family.

Too fat.

Too skinny.

Too short.

Too tall.

Wrong hair color.

No hair of any color.

Not athletic.

Broken home.

Bad health.

Disability.

Not being happy and content with the hand we've been dealt leaves deep wounds in our lives. Who's to blame for these wounds? Who made all of this happen?

Sometimes it's us.

Sometimes it's others.

Sometimes we blame God.

Whether it's consciously or subconsciously done, our unhappiness is blamed on someone or something else. And that unhappiness starts to manifest itself into something we're more familiar saying than understanding: insecurity.

Insecurity.

Mistrust.

Feelings of vulnerability.

A deep suspicion of who we are, what we are, and where we are.

Judgment of our self-image.

Bruises to our ego.

Insecurity is best defined in the negative—what it's *not.*

For instance, insecurity is *not* security.

Security is the feeling of safety. Contentment. Trust. Peace of mind. Happiness. Confidence of an outcome.

We strive in all ways to make things secure around

us. If our environment isn't secure, we work to change it—or we embrace the restlessness of not being secure.

If you live in a neighborhood you consider safe, you can leave the front door of your house unlocked. You feel secure, knowing your house is safe. If that feeling of security changed—for instance, if someone's house down the street were broken into—your feeling of security would turn into mistrust. To elevate your feelings of security in that case, then, you'd lock your front door, the garage door, and the glass door that leads to the porch.

If locking your doors didn't fix your feeling of security, you'd make adjustments again to try to fix that feeling of mistrust.

You might get deadbolts for the doors.

If that didn't fix your feelings, you might buy an alarm system.

If that didn't fix your feelings, you might move to a new house in a new neighborhood.

If that didn't fix your feelings, you might never answer the door or leave the house.

Cal Ripken Jr.'s mother was abducted at gunpoint and held for twenty-three hours by an unknown assailant. On the television show *Good Morning America* Ripken told viewers his mother was so shaken up, she refused to go back her house—a house where she'd lived for nearly fifty years!

"Her sense of security is violated," Ripken had said.[2]

If our feeling of security is threatened or diminished, we add new barriers to insulate and cover ourselves in order to make ourselves feel the way we think we should feel, had there not been a breach in the security we once felt in the first place.

A nice way to say it is that we develop defense mechanisms—additions and changes to who we are to bolster our sense of security.

Defense mechanisms are not healthy ways of living. They're masks we put on to make ourselves feel more secure. This isn't security. It's self-manipulation of the feeling of security.

Think about it.

Anyone, at any time, can get through that glass door on your patio. The security device on that glass door is so poor, it can be breached by accident—by an inconspicuous rock under your mower deck or a baseball that bounces off the top of a baseball glove.

Defense mechanisms are a naive reach for an imagined sense of true and pure contentment. They are, ultimately, unhealthy ways of living that bring more damage to ourselves and others over time. They're not natural because of the unhealthy by-products they contain.

When we put up defense mechanisms, we're attempting to free ourselves from the feeling of a lack of security, peace, or trust. We want desperately to be free from those feelings that we'll do anything to change them.

Our attempts to do this usually happen below the surface—in, as doctors call it, your subconscious—but you'll see it penetrate your everyday life and your conscious way of thinking too. Your defense mechanisms become your self-seeking reach for freedom from insecurity.

That was deep.

I know.

But if you're honest, you know what I mean.

And they say the first step to overcoming anything is self-realization.

Do they say that?

They should.

Socrates famously said, "Know thyself."

At least, the phrase sounds so wise, it's attributed to Socrates.

So I'll just go ahead and level with you. Jacob's story is my story. I walked clothed with insecurity for far too long. It's changing now—I've come to the point of knowing those insecurities. Of admitting them. Of beginning to break free of them.

And the same can be true for you.

This book isn't a frolic through flowery fields of feel-good words. It's a wrestle through our identity questions and finally realizing who we are and are meant to be.

And you take the first step by being honest with yourself about your discontentment and insecurity.

It Begins With Honesty

Your sense of insecurity probably developed long before you were aware it was happening.

Maybe it developed in your early childhood. Erik Erikson, the famous professor who studied social behavior and is most known for coining the phrase "identity crisis," believed that the stem of our insecurities can be traced back to our first developmental period of life: our childhood.[3]

Erikson's studies helped me understand my own insecurities.

I grew up in a broken home. I don't remember my parents ever living together. I have vague memories of a duplex house off the Rocky Mountains where I played baseball with my dad in the backyard with a giant oversized bat and plastic ball. Other than that memory, though, my childhood was a ping-pong experience of bouncing from one parent to the next.

My parents remarried and started new families before I entered first grade.

Here I was, the odd man out.

The third wheel.

The firstborn, but really an also-ran.

Jake.

My mom's new husband had a German pride thing

going for him. His last name was Wetzler. I was the oldest child in the family, but I wasn't his, and I wasn't a Wetzler. I remember him telling me once, "You are not my son." How could I ever feel I was part of the family when I was being told I wasn't?

My dad's new wife was young and ready to start her new life—new family, new car, new house, new everything. She got all of that with my dad, and I was a remnant of his former life—surely hard for any twentysomething wife to swallow into her dreams.

Lonely was an understatement.

I got lost in books, in making people laugh, and in make-believe games. All my make-believe dreams were focused on people wanting me and being proud of me.

I realize now that was because of the insecurities I felt in my life.

Grade school didn't help with those insecurities either.

My mom and stepdad moved me to Italy when I was six years old. Now I wasn't just the kid who didn't fit in with his family. I was also the kid who didn't fit in with the culture around him.

There was this one boy named Luigi. (This was long before the Mario Brothers and Nintendo made the name Luigi synonymous with green overalls and plumbing.) Luigi had a habit of making sure I wouldn't fit in with the Italian kids. He picked on me—we called it bullying in those days—because I was the skinniest kid in my grade and had lips and ears I hadn't grown into yet. I was always getting taller, which made playing sports tough in grade school. Walking around like a baby giraffe is a pain for a boy trying to be what boys try to be. Luigi was a great soccer player, and he was constantly trying to get me to play, only to prove that I was not as good as he was.

I'm sure if you took the time, you could think back to your own early childhood years and find circumstances and events that shaped your sense of insecurity and mistrust too.

Maybe it developed years after your childhood.

Maybe it's just part of what it means to be human.

Maybe it's what biblical writers described as our "flesh."

Maybe it's because of those curses that come down to us from the beginning of humanity, meaning we're just born with it. I can't help but read the account of Adam and Eve in the Book of Genesis and see that we, as humans, live with a curse that is very specific to men and women.

Whenever the insecurity started for you, I have no doubt it's painful to relive, realize, trace back, and think through.

But I will tell you this.

If you don't take the first step to realize it's there, your insecurity will sabotage your life. This war that rages inside each one of us can—and will—destroy us from the inside out, and the sad thing is, the majority of us will never recognize it, much less admit it.

Your insecurity and my insecurity work against us living the life God has for us.

INSECURITY BREEDS SABOTAGE

Let me show you how.

In Luke 10 the medical doctor Luke tells a story about a lawyer who approaches Jesus one day and asks how he can have eternal life.

In law school we call the way Jesus responds to the lawyer's question the "Socratic method"—the teacher asks questions in response to the questions asked by a student in order to keep the pupil articulating thoughts and ideas in search of the answer. This is just what Jesus does. He turns around and asks a question right back: "What do the sacred scriptures say about this? How do you read it?"

This lawyer thinks for a minute and then answers back, quoting Deuteronomy 6:5: "You shall love the Lord your God with all your heart and with all your soul and with all your strength and with all your mind, and your neighbor as yourself" (Luke 10:27).

Jesus applauds the lawyer's answer, saying, "You have answered correctly; do this, and you will live" (v. 28).

Let's unpack this before we go any further.

The lawyer's answer can be outlined into three areas.

Love God.

Love others.

Love ourselves.

And not just love in the sense of having good feelings toward someone, but love that is characterized as being all of who we are—heart, soul, strength, and mind. Think about it in these terms: our feelings, our being, our effort, and our thoughts.

Jesus can be understood as saying here that to truly live is to do these things. To truly live the life that is possible, we need to strive for these types of loving relationships.

But here is the thing about insecurity.

It sabotages all of that.

Remember, consciously or subconsciously, someone or something is to blame for all our mistrust, our situations, the hand we've been dealt.

Those wounds have a perpetrator.

How can you and I fully love God with all our feelings, all our being, all our effort, and all our thoughts when we're blaming Him for what makes us unhappy?

How can you and I fully love others when we're blaming them for our unhappiness?

How can you and I fully love ourselves when we're not even happy with ourselves?

Let's put it another way.

How can I truly love my parents when deep inside I harbor resentment for the feelings I felt as a kid growing up?

How can I truly love the people around me when I blame them and society for making me feel ugly and like I don't fit in?

How can I truly love myself when I'm not happy with what I am or what I have?

If the foundation of each of these relationships is built on mistrust and discontentment, how is it ever going to be possible to experience healthy relationships and a complete life?

It isn't.

That's the point.

Eventually the insecurity at the base of it all will bubble up from the foundation and rear its ugly head in each area of our lives. It sabotages the life Jesus says will make us truly *live*.

Makes you look at Jacob's story a little differently, doesn't it?

BECOMING WHO WE AREN'T

Remember our boy, Jake.

So unhappy with who he is.

Not the oldest son.

Not the one through whom God's blessing was promised to come.

Jacob is willing to sabotage it all through his

insecurity. He hatches a plan—the first leg of which is to steal his brother's birthright.

Based on the customs of this time period, Jacob's older brother, Esau, would receive two portions of the inheritance when Isaac died. Jacob, being the younger son, would receive one.

Jacob is not happy with this.

He watches his brother.

Learns his habits.

Learns what drives him.

Learns where he's weak.

Then executes part one of his plan.

One day Esau goes out to work in the field, just as he does every day. Jacob, knowing when his brother would come in from the field and how hungry his brother is when he comes in, decides to make a stew at that exact time.

Sure enough, Esau comes in tired and hungry.

He sees the stew Jacob is making and demands to eat of it.

Jacob takes advantage of this situation and agrees— for a small fee.

Esau's birthright.

Esau's double-portion of the inheritance.

Jacob knows his twin brother is a passionate man.

An impulsive man.

An impatient man.

An extremely hairy man.

And while we might not ever understand why Esau agrees at that moment to give his inheritance to Jacob for a measly bowl of stew, that's exactly what he does.

Jacob has completed part one of his plan. As the younger brother, he will get not only one portion of the inheritance from his dad, but he will also get his older brother's inheritance as well.

Now Jacob hatches part two of his plan.

He has to wait until his father is close to death before it can be played out.

And that day does come.

When Jacob's father, Isaac, reaches a frail age and can't see very well anymore, Jacob executes his next sting operation. His plan is to trick his father into giving him the blessings God promised this great family of theirs—the blessing that was suppose to be passed down to the oldest son, Esau.

How will Jacob convince his father that he is Esau, a skillful hunter, a hairy man's man?

Esau must have been a lot hairier than I can imagine, because Jacob takes animal fur and puts it on his arms and legs to mimic the hairiness of his older brother. He then puts his brother's clothes on, so he smells like him. (Apparently they wore different cologne.)

Then he goes to his father, Isaac, and in Genesis 27, we see the whole story unfold.

When Jacob, dressed as Esau, approaches his father, Isaac asks, "Who are you?" (v. 18).

Jacob responds by saying, "I am Esau your firstborn" (v. 19).

Now, in Jewish writing, the details of a story are important to the whole story. They skip details and dialogue that aren't important to the overall story. Particularly they make sure the first words recorded are of the utmost importance.

Isaac's first words to Jacob are, "Who are you?"

Jacob's first words are, "I am Esau, your firstborn."

You can call this foreshadowing, but there is something bigger going on here.

We are introduced to Jacob in the Book of Genesis only two other times before we read this story. The first is Jacob's birth story, where he is trying to stop his brother from being born first. The second is the story of him tricking his brother into giving him his birthright for a bowl of stew.

Think about it.

Every story so far is about Jacob not wanting the life he's been given—not liking who he is and instead wanting what his brother has.

And the first words we have in this story too have to do with Jacob not wanting to be Jacob.

In fact, he's actually pretending to be someone else.

It's the first identity theft in recorded history.

Jacob's dad, Isaac, isn't buying it at first, though.

I mean, the voice he hears is Jacob's voice. Isaac's eyesight is shot, and he has to rely on his other senses to detect if this boy is who he says he is. So when he hears Jacob's voice, he questions Jacob immediately.

Jacob reassures his dad that he is Esau.

Now, the text says Isaac's eyes were "dim" (v. 1). There's a sense here that he wasn't completely blind. I've often wondered if Esau and Jacob, being twins, were similar in appearance, making it even harder for Isaac to distinguish between the two with his already failing eyesight. We know the text says how hairy and red Esau was, but that doesn't mean they couldn't have been very similar in appearance otherwise.

In any case, Jake convinces his dad that he's Esau.

The animal fur and clothes swap work.

And Isaac blesses Jacob, thinking Jacob is Esau, with the blessing God promised to this celebrated family.

Jacob has succeeded in not being the second-born son. He's taken all that is his brother's. The life he didn't want has been swapped for a cheap imitation made of animal fur, smelly clothes, and careful trickery.

But again, this story isn't just Jacob's story.

It's our story. It's the story of how our insecurity sabotages us from truly living.

And so the sabotage begins.

Chapter 2

MEMORIAL OF PRIDE

Try not to become a man of success, but
rather try to become a man of value.[1]

—ALBERT EINSTEIN

A FEW YEARS INTO my church-planting experience in Utah and the missionary work I oversaw there, I found myself traveling around the country to speak at other churches and events about what we were doing in Utah. This wasn't too unusual, as this was how I had raised the necessary funds to start the work in Utah in the first place. But when I was raising money for the initial effort, I had to beg for that "ten-minute window"—that infamously boring segment of time in a church service buried between announcements and the offering. Now, pastors and church leaders were inviting me to speak. I was no longer a beggar.

On one occasion I was super excited about the opportunity to speak and tell our story to a very large church, but it became one of the most embarrassing moments of my life.

First, I got off the plane to find someone holding a sign at the baggage claim that said, "Mr. Jordan." I was told someone was going to pick me up, but I wasn't expecting an actual driver! I headed toward the sign-holding driver, and when I was five feet away, someone else got to him first. The driver put his sign down, grabbed the guy's bag, and they headed out of the airport.

I stopped dead in my tracks.

I looked down at the floor, trying to comprehend what had just happened.

Was my last name Jordan?

Did I miss any instructions from the church?

Next thing I knew, my phone rang. It was someone from the church giving me directions to where they were parked so we could head to the hotel.

Feeling sheepish about the awkward moment at baggage claim, I have to admit that I walked into my hotel room a little despondent. While I had not expected a driver before I arrived, once the idea of a driver presented itself, I thought having one might be nice.

My spirits were lifted when I saw a big gift basket sitting on the desk of the hotel room. You might not admit it, but I will: I like to be honored by others. It feels good to be thought worthy to be showered with gifts. That gift basket made me feel a bit better after my embarrassing *faux pas* at the airport.

The next morning, as I sat on the front row of the church, waiting for my time to speak, I read through the bulletin for the morning's events. It was a Sunday dedicated to missionary efforts around the United States and the world, and there was a little paragraph about me as their guest speaker. But what caught my eye was the event listed right before my turn to speak. It said, "Presentation of Our Annual Missions Gift."

I thought that sounded interesting.

I had no clue what it was, though.

When we reached that unknown part of the event, a leader in the church got up and started to talk.

"We have with us a special guest," he said. "A guest

that has flown in to be here with us. Our guest is a one-of-a-kind missionary. A missionary to a place that is hard to start churches. A missionary to a place that others don't want to go. A missionary that has inspired us, and we feel we are to present to them our financial gift that we saved up all year to give to that one missions project that we feel we need to partner with. It is with great honor that I present to you ... "

The whole time he was talking, I was swelling with excitement.

"They didn't tell me they were doing this for me," I thought. "This is a huge church. If they have been saving all year for this, this is going to be the biggest financial gift we have ever received!"

The smile on my face would not go away.

As the presenter got to the point where he was about to present me, my legs kicked into autopilot and moved on their own. I started to stand as he finished.

" ... John and Jane Doe, missionaries to Africa."

Here I was, standing, just as they were announcing someone else's name.

The couple right behind me stood a few seconds after I did and made their way to the front of the stage. Someone from the side of the stage began walking out an oversized check like you get when you win the lottery.

My reflexes made me stand when I didn't want to, but they also kicked in to save my pride in that moment.

24

I had turned to see the couple stand behind me, and I immediately started clapping. This led to the whole congregation standing and applauding. I became the suave guest who led a church in a standing ovation—a real humble leader, swelling with pride for my African compatriots.

I am not sure what this missionary couple said as they were on the stage. I sat down, my face burning red, and began to pray.

What was going on with me?

What had happened inside of me that made me think everything was about me?

Why was I so prideful?

This was not you, Trinity.

Why now?

Where did all this come from?

I wish I could say when it was my time to speak, I confessed my pride to the audience that day.

But I didn't.

I was too chicken.

On the flight home, though, I made a vow.

I would not build memorials to myself.

I knew if I started to build memorials to myself, even if just in my mind, then I would sabotage the life God had for me. I would rather look like I was owed nothing than look like I was owed anything.

That is what insecurity does to us—makes us think everything's about us.

It's Not About You

It all goes back to those defense mechanisms we talked about. When we are not 100 percent secure in who we are, then we will alter our behavior so as to alter our security level. And one of those alterations, or defense mechanisms, is making things all about us.

If the first step to overcoming the sabotage of insecurity is to realize we have insecurities in the first place, then the second step to overcoming sabotage is to realize this world isn't about us.

Without this realization we start living in a way that keeps us from being happy with our lives, our circumstances, and the very people we were created to be.

I mean, if this is about me, how can I be happy if I don't get what I want?

You see this way of thinking in small children. They have an almost natural tendency to make things about them. They go to a birthday party and get upset they didn't get a present. They go to the store and want you to buy them something and then get upset when you don't.

It can be easy to watch small children make life about themselves at times. It can be easy to see it in others.

It's hard to see that same tendency in ourselves, though.

It's almost as if we live our lives trying to erect memorials to ourselves while demolishing the memorials others have built to themselves.

But this world isn't about us.

It isn't about you.

It isn't about me.

And if life *isn't* about me, then my happiness in myself and my life isn't based on what I have received or not received.

It isn't about what I've accomplished or not accomplished.

It isn't about my memorial.

One of the reasons we see things as being about us is that we see things only from our own perspective. If we could see things from God's perspective, it would be easy to see this isn't about us. Only God has the view of seeing the big picture of eternity.

In the Book of Isaiah the prophet speaks for God and writes this on God's behalf: "I am God, and there is no other; I am God, and there is none like me, declaring the end from the beginning and from ancient times things not yet done, saying, 'My counsel shall stand, and I will accomplish all my purposes'" (Isa. 46:9–10).

God knows the beginning.

God knows the end.

And God's purposes are the ones played out in this world.

Only God's purposes.

Not ours.

You can't see it though. I can't see it either. Our perspective in life is limited and incomplete.

You are the created.

You are not the Creator.

You were created by a Creator for His purposes and will, not yours.

The Ingredients None of Us Want to Taste

One of my favorite books in all of the Bible is the Book of Ecclesiastes. It's not a very popular book to read for the reason of its being a little dark and not very cheerful. In fact, I did a series of teachings on Ecclesiastes once and someone came up to me, saying, "Why on earth would you want to study this depressing book with everyone?"

I love the Book of Ecclesiastes because it's written with wisdom by someone who has been there and done that. Solomon was the king of Israel, and he had it all. I mean, *he had it all.*

He was the richest guy around—like Bill Gates for his time period.

He owned everything—think Donald Trump here.

He controlled one of if not *the* most powerful nations at the time—think military powerhouse.

He ate the finest foods—think Gordon Ramsey.

He drank the finest drinks.

There wasn't anything he didn't have or hadn't tried.

He had three hundred wives—think *The Real Housewives of Israel* but all of them having the same husband.

He had seven hundred girlfriends—meaning he was either the ultimate lady's man or a complete moron.

He had it *all*—whatever he wanted, whenever he wanted, however he wanted.

And because of all that he learned some vital lessons that he passed down in the Book of Ecclesiastes.

The reason I love the book is because you don't take advice from someone who hasn't been there. You can study a subject for years under a teacher who has also studied for years—some pedigreed genius—but the person I want to hear from is the guy who has actually experienced it.

This is the Book of Ecclesiastes.

In chapter 3 of the book there's this chunk of writing. You've probably heard it before. It reads kind of like a laundry list:

> For everything there is a season, and a time
>   for every matter under heaven:
> a time to be born, and a time to die;

> a time to plant, and a time to pluck up what
> is planted;
> a time to kill, and a time to heal;
> a time to break down, and a time to build up;
> a time to weep, and a time to laugh;
> a time to mourn, and a time to dance;
> a time to cast away stones, and a time to
> gather stones together;
> a time to embrace, and a time to refrain from
> embracing;
> a time to seek, and a time to lose;
> a time to keep, and a time to cast away;
> a time to tear, and a time to sew;
> a time to keep silence, and a time to speak;
> a time to love, and a time to hate;
> a time for war, and a time for peace.
> —ECCLESIASTES 3:1–8

Solomon, in all his wisdom, in all that he'd observed and experienced, wrote out this list for us. It's a list many have taken to be things that can occur in life, but Solomon pushes us a little deeper than just building a list of possible things you *might* face. He writes this out to say these *are* the things God puts in our lives to make us into who we are supposed to be and to fulfill His purpose.

I heard a pastor say once to think of it as ingredients— this is a list of things God mixes together to serve a bigger purpose than you and I can ever understand.

Let's be honest.

That stinks.

It's terrifying.

A time to break down? A time to cast away stones? What does that even mean?

I don't want some of those things on that list to be mixed into my life. I don't care if it will benefit me. I don't care if it serves a bigger purpose that I can't see.

I want to pick the ingredients of my life.

And if you're honest, you want to pick the ingredients of your life too.

But here's the thing. The *right* ingredients, blended together, make the best recipes possible.

There's a story that circulates in my family about when my parents were first married. They married when they were still teenagers, and my mom hadn't really learned to do any cooking in her family because she was the youngest girl.

When my parents celebrated their first fall season together, my mom decided to make my dad a pumpkin pie. She had never made a pumpkin pie before.

But how hard could it be?

You buy the piecrust, you buy the pumpkin pie mix in the can, and you cook it, right?

Well, that is exactly what she did. She added nothing to the can mix—just poured it in the piecrust and popped it in the oven.

My dad says it was the worst thing he has ever tasted.

So, you need all the right ingredients to make

something taste right. And this list Solomon gives us has the ingredients God uses, then mixes together in our lives to make us into the people He wants us to be for a bigger outcome than you and I can see from our limited perspective.

We don't get to pick the ingredients for our lives.

God does.

If I gave my kids nothing but goodies and treats without making them eat their vegetables that they don't like, they would grow up unhealthy. In the same way, God has a plan for you and loves you too much to just give you all the good things in life and not mix into your life the things that taste bland, bitter, or even bad sometimes.

Here is where you have to go next in your understanding of the insecurities that sabotage us: God is about the business of growing you into who He created you to be, yes, but this isn't about you.

That's a paradox.

A dichotomy.

This isn't about you.

It's about God.

An eternal God who sees all things, knows all things, works out all things, and created all things. We use the word *sovereign* to describe this concept that God is not controlled by anyone and that He is about His business, working out a great plan we cannot see.

You don't have the eternal perspective He does.

Let's be honest though.

We are self-centered.

We would rather pick the ingredients of life than let God pick them.

We instinctively make this about us every single time.

MEMORIAL-MAKING IN OUR OWN NAME

Jacob walked this same path too.

After Jake stole his brother's identity and then his blessing, Esau is upset. Actually, *upset* is probably an understatement. Esau is so mad that he begins plotting Jacob's death.

Rebekah, Jacob's mom, finds out about her son wanting to kill his brother and convinces Isaac to send Jacob off to find a wife in a faraway land. So Jacob begins his wife-finding journey, which really is a journey to his relative's house. It was like going to a family reunion to find a wife.

Not long into this wife journey Jacob reaches a certain place and stops to rest for the night. Genesis 28 tells us that he finds a stone and uses it for a pillow. And maybe because he was using a stone for a pillow, Jacob ends up having a crazy dream.

In his dream Jacob sees angels all over the place, and in the middle of all the angels is God. God begins to deliver this proclamation of what He is promising to Jacob in his life:

> I am the Lord.
> I am the God of your grandfather and father.
> You will rule over the very land you sleep on.
> Your descendants will rule over the very land
>   you sleep on.
> You will have lots of descendants.
> Your descendants will bless all the families of
>   the world.
> I am going to be with you wherever you go.
> I am going to take care of you wherever you
>   go.
> And I will not leave you.
> —Genesis 28:13–15, author's paraphrase

Jacob awakes in fear.

Fear because all those stories he grew up hearing about his grandfather and father having these "God moments" are now at his own doorstep.

Fear because he hasn't been honoring God up to this point.

Fear because God is declaring what God wants to do and not what Jacob wants to do.

Hard, cold fear.

So Jacob decides to do something with this vision from God and this moment of fear. He wants to remember this "God moment," and he wants to control the situation. So he does two things.

First, he takes the stone he used for a pillow and sets it up vertically in the ground. There was a common practice in his time to set up a memorial to an event. And that is exactly what he means to do.

He will erect a pillar, pour oil over it, and give it a name.

This will be a memorial—a place to remember what God had shown him and said to him.

Memorials are not foreign to us. We have lots of them. Washington DC is full of them. Lincoln Memorial. Washington Memorial. Jefferson Memorial. Vietnam Veterans Memorial.

Your city probably has smaller memorials—parks, buildings, or streets named for people worth remembering. These are places we go to ponder, think, and remember the events or people the memorials are all about.

So Jacob sets up this memorial. He names it Bethel, which means "house of God."

Here is where Jacob saw angels ascending and descending into heaven.

Where God was seen.

Where God spoke to Jacob.

Jacob doesn't want to forget this place or this event.

It's significant.

And then, second—because Jacob wants to pick his ingredients, just like we all do—he tries to strike a deal with God.

This is basically what he says:

> If God will be with *me*...
> If God will keep *me* in the way *I* want to
> go...
> If God will give *me* food and clothing...
> *then* this God will truly be my God.
> —GENESIS 28:20–22, AUTHOR PARAPHRASE

If you take any logic class, you'll learn about "if-then" statements. If A happens, then B happens. So Jacob picks some major ingredients and says in his prayer that *if* God gives him these specific ingredients of life, *then* he will honor God.

Let's stop here for a moment.

Isn't that trying to control God?

Don't we already see that God's will and purpose will be done? God is sovereign, unaffected by anyone or anything, and yet Jacob assumes a bargainer's position.

Of course, this is unfamiliar to us, right?

No.

We've all done something similar, haven't we?

We've struck a bargain.

"God, if You do _____, then I will never do _____ again."

This is a bargain based on manipulation. *I will only do something if You will give me what I want.* We've tried this with God, and so has Jacob!

Now, Jacob is one of our Bible heroes, right? Doesn't that bargaining behavior seem unlike anything we've ever been taught about our Bible heroes? Jacob can't be a spoiled, selfish, self-centered, prideful person, thinking he can change God...can he?

Yes, he can.

He is.

He doesn't like that he was second-born.

He tricked others into giving him something that wasn't his to have.

And now he's making self-centered requests to God and telling God that if he doesn't get what he wants, then perhaps there are other gods to serve—gods whose paths are cleaner and make more sense.

I wonder if this memorial of Jacob had more to do with the vow he was making with God than the vision he received. I wonder if this was the spot, in Jacob's mind, where he would always remember what God owed him and what he, in return, would give to God.

The memorial might seem to point to an ephemeral staircase populated with angels, but I think it might actually have been a memorial of pride. "This is where *I* saw the staircase of angels," you can just hear Jacob thinking. Then, "Not Abraham. Not Isaac."

Instead of seeing the perspective of God's eternal purpose being fulfilled, all Jacob can see is what's in it for him. He had taken Esau's identity and blessing, and now God would give him even more.

Insecurity will do that to you.

If you aren't happy with you, all you'll care about

is you. You'll only worry about what ingredients God gives you and what memorial you're building to yourself. You'll only care about what good things you get. It'll sting when things don't go the way you thought they should. It'll hurt when bad things cross your path.

You.

You.

You.

You.

You.

At the root of insecurity is a focus on ourselves.

And if you look around, you'll see that society as a whole is caught up in this perspective. People think that by fulfilling a desire inside of themselves, they'll find the freedom they were always looking for—freedom from whatever is causing their insecurity.

We live our lives with the perspective that if we get to the next level of life...

Or reach a goal...

Or get that job...

Or finally find that type of girl or guy...

Or own this type of house...

Or secure this amount of fame...

Then there will be joy and happiness.

Insecurities gone.

Freedom achieved.

This is our society's perspective.

And you know as well as I do that when you get to that level, meet that goal, or hit that achievement that would bring you freedom, it doesn't bring it. Our desire and focus on ourselves just bring us to new levels of wanting even more—wanting the next level beyond where we just got—because freedom wasn't where we thought it would be.

Life will teach you that this self-seeking, you-type living leaves a wake of destruction in our hearts and in the lives of those around us.

If our perspective doesn't change, our insecurities never will either.

This is not about us.

You have to put yourself to death, and not just one time but constantly—for the rest of your life. And sometimes you'll put yourself to death and wake up in the morning to find that self came back with his brother.

And so you'll have to do it all again.

If you don't, you'll find yourself erecting memorials of pride, and you'll eventually find those memorials don't fix anything.

But, hey. This isn't about you. And it isn't about Jacob either.

Let's keep on discovering why.

PART II

SEPARATION

Chapter 3

WHAT IS THAT TO YOU?

If you're always striving to achieve a success that is defined by someone else, I think you'll always be frustrated....Define your own success.[1]

—COACH K, LEGENDARY BASKETBALL COACH

J ACOB'S STORY IS far from the only story of insecurity in the Bible. But I think it's easy to read the pages of the Bible and miss that. Our tendency is to place the writers and characters on pedestals and assume they don't have flaws in the same manner we do. The records of Jacob and his family members are in the Bible—clearly they are the protagonists. Biblical protagonists are seen as different—less flawed—than other kinds of historical or literary heroes. Shakespearean heroes are flawed. Odysseus was flawed. Even modern writers of memoirs show their flaws. But somehow it seems sacrosanct to attach flaws to biblical characters, except if they are obvious bad guys. We see their stories as wonderful events of history that will never be duplicated in our lives—no struggles, no problems, no drama, and no turmoil. The struggles that do exist are either easily solved or—better—God solves their dilemmas Himself.

Maybe we are reading the pages of the Bible with a bias of glamorized Sunday school affection.

Maybe we are hoping these others, because their histories are housed in our holy book, are superhuman.

Maybe we read too fast.

Maybe it's a combination of all these things.

I'm convinced that if we would slow down and remember that every person who wrote and stars in the Bible was human like you and me, then we would start to see the real picture flow out of the text.

We would start to see they lived the same type of life you and I are living.

We would start to see their humanity.

We would start to see their struggles.

We would start to see we are no different than they were.

A hero, just like those of us who are not yet heroes, stumbles into conflict based on personality quirks, poor decisions, and, yes, sin.

For instance.

A Little Disciple-ish Rivalry

In John 20 the story of Jesus rising from the grave after His death on the cross starts to play itself out. If you remember the story, John writes that Mary Magdalene went to the tomb where Jesus's body was laid early in the morning on the day Jesus rose from the grave. She discovered His body was missing and, thinking someone had stolen His body, ran to tell the disciples.

This is how John records whom she told:

> So she ran and went to Simon Peter and the other disciple, the one whom Jesus loved, and said to them, "They have taken the Lord out of the tomb, and we do not know where they have laid him."
>
> —John 20:2

Now, during this time period, when someone was writing a narrative history of events, it wasn't uncommon for the writer not to identify himself in the narrative with personal pronouns. The writer would normally come up with a way to identify himself so others would know whom they were talking about, usually by using a descriptive phrase that would key everyone in on who they were in the story.

John has done this.

In fact, he picks a descriptive phrase to distinguish himself in the story that elevates himself among all of Jesus's followers.

He chooses to call himself "the one whom Jesus loved."

Maybe he could have said that about *all* of Jesus's disciples, but he doesn't. He singles himself out as "the *one*"—not "one of many" or "one of twelve" or "someone who," but "the *one*."

In this instance of narrative, the phrase reads as a knock on Peter. John is telling us the events of Jesus's resurrection, and he tells us there's Peter and then there's "the one whom Jesus loved."

Plain ol' Pete and…(trumpets sounding)…Jesus's favorite.

John's writing was the last to be written amongst the disciples of Jesus. Maybe since he was last to write his book of events, he felt it was easier to give himself such a grand descriptive title. All the other disciples were dead at this point. There was no one to argue with him and no one to offend.

Back where we left off in John's telling of the resurrection story, he writes:

> So Peter went out with the other disciple, and they were going toward the tomb. Both of them were running together, but the other disciple outran Peter and reached the tomb first. And stooping to look in, he saw the linen cloths lying there, but he did not go in. Then Simon Peter came, following him, and went into the tomb. He saw the linen cloths lying there, and the face cloth, which had been on Jesus' head, not lying with the linen cloths but folded up in a place by itself. Then the other disciple, who had reached the tomb first, also went in, and he saw and believed.
>
> —JOHN 20:3–8

Don't read too fast here.

Do you see it?

John makes sure he points out he is a faster runner than Peter—that he gets to the tomb first.

And, unlike Peter, that he believed in the resurrection right away.

If you are going to write the account of your experience with Jesus, why not tell everyone how much better you are than someone like Peter?

Peter was the oldest disciple.

The take-charge guy.

Why not show everyone *you* were the one Jesus loved, the one who could outrun the older guy, the one who believed first in the resurrection?

Well, that is exactly what John does in writing his story.

Here it is—the whole reason we, as followers of Jesus, have a hope for the future and life. The reconciliation of man and God. The crescendo of human history. And woven into this powerful story of death conquered is a petty rivalry between Peter and John.

You don't buy it?

Let me show you more.

In the last chapter of John's Gospel narrative, he writes of one of the last moments the disciples get to spend physical time with Jesus after He has revealed Himself to them. They're eating breakfast on the banks of the Sea of Galilee, and Jesus begins to tell Peter some very amazing things:

> When they had finished breakfast, Jesus said to Simon Peter, "Simon, son of John, do you love me more than these?" He said to him, "Yes, Lord; you know that I love you." He said to him, "Feed my lambs." He said to him a second time, "Simon, son of John, do you love me?" He said to him, "Yes, Lord; you know that I love you." He said to him "Tend my sheep."

He said to him the third time, "Simon, son of John, do you love me?" Peter was grieved because he said to him the third time, "Do you love me?" and he said to him, "Lord, you know everything; you know that I love you." Jesus said to him, "Feed my sheep."

—John 21:15–17

Jesus is not only antagonizing Peter, maybe since Peter denied Him three times, but He is also revealing to Peter what Jesus has in store for his life. Jesus is showing Peter his deep purpose for it. Peter is going to lead Jesus's sheep. He is going to shepherd those who follow after Jesus. He is going to look after those Jesus once looked after.

This is Peter's abundant, unique life. It's what Peter is supposed to be and do.

But look what happens next:

Peter turned and saw the disciple whom Jesus loved following them, the one who also had leaned back against him during the supper and had said, "Lord, who is it that is going to betray you?" When Peter saw him, he said to Jesus, "Lord, what about this man?"

—John 21:20–21

John doesn't care that we are in the middle of a great moment in Peter's life, where Jesus is revealing deep truths of Peter's life to him. Instead, John wants you to know he's even more than just "the one whom Jesus loved"—he's also the one who leaned against Jesus during the Last Supper. He's the one who asked Jesus who was going to be the betrayer.

Notice John is still comparing himself to Peter in petty ways here, showing us how awesome he is, but also revealing to us he was following Peter and Jesus as they walked down the beach and had this intimate conversation. John has to tell us he was spying on their conversation so he can record what Peter said to Jesus and Jesus's response.

And look at Peter.

He sees John following him and Jesus, and all he can think is, "What does that guy get?"

Here's a moment all of us would want with Jesus—a moment where Jesus is laying out what He has in store for Peter's life. And all Peter can think is, "What about him?"

You know how this is, don't you?

I do.

We measure and compare because we're not secure with who we are or what we have.

"Maybe God is giving me the short end of the stick."

"Maybe I'll be happier with what that guy has."

"Maybe my unhappiness has to do with not having what they have—they look so happy."

"In fact, maybe they're the reason I'm unhappy—they took what could have been mine!"

Really, we're still making it about us.

And when we make it about us, a lot of things happen—or don't happen.

We never connect with those around us the way God intended us to connect with them.

We never love them the way that God intended us to love them.

We live our lives trying to pull others down to have less than us so we end up winning the comparison game or running on a treadmill, trying to get more and more and more, in order to keep up with those who seem to have more than we do.

In all of these cases, comparisons sabotage our lives.

Even the most petty rivalries cause destruction.

Petty.

You don't have petty rivalries, do you?

Yes, you do.

I'll tell you about one of mine. When I was a kid, we moved a lot—mainly because I bounced from parent to parent, but also because my stepdad's job caused us to move every few years.

When I moved to Sacramento at the beginning of junior high, I saw that the "in" thing was to wear big Starter brand coats and hats. I had a Kmart special coat, and the kids around me made sure to let me know how uncool my coat was compared to their Starter coats.

My mom went out with my request for a Starter coat that would make me just like everyone else and bought me a Mighty Ducks Starter coat. It was on sale. (Of course it was on sale. It was a brand-new team named the Mighty Ducks!)

I was trying so hard to fit in with the new kids in our new city, and here I was, walking around with a dorky Mighty Ducks Starter coat.

I got the right brand. Not the right team.

I tried to wear it with pride, though. I really did. At least for my mom's sake.

A 49ers or Raiders coat could have saved my early teen years. Instead, I was derailed by an Emilio Estevez's movie and a Disney decision to branch out into professional sports. Quack.

Then I moved to Utah.

In Utah it was a vastly different scenario in terms of what was cool. Reebok pump shoes, Guess jeans, and overalls were all the rage.

I took my requests to my parents.

The pump shoes didn't end up an accessory item in my wardrobe, due to their cost, but I did snag some Guess jeans overalls. Of course, you couldn't wear both overall straps—this was form over function, and you didn't want to look like you were working the farm. And thanks to hip-hop groups such as Kris Kross, this meant you had to hang one of the straps down, undone, or hook both straps like they were going to be on your shoulders but instead hung down off of them.

This is what the kids in Utah were using to compare and decide who was cool and who was not.

Then I moved to Arkansas.

I expected to wear those same overalls, just with a piece of hay sticking out of my mouth. Nope. Ralph Lauren and Tommy Hilfiger polo shirts were the style in Arkansas at the time. (Perhaps dressing preppy was a form of Southern rebellion.)

I was able to go shopping with my mom this time, so we didn't have a repeat of the Mighty Ducks fiasco. I ended up with a few shirts that granted me favor with the new purveyors of cool. I wore those few shirts out trying to stay in the cool crowd.

Now, thinking back to those years of trying to fit in with my peers based on an arbitrary style of clothing makes me realize how petty all of it was.

Yet we still strive to appear fashionable.

Admit it.

There are clothes you would not be caught dead wearing because of what others would think of you. Or stores you won't shop in because of the social stigma that would get attached to you.

In our age no one is impervious to fashion trends—even pastors.

Especially pastors.

Just a generation ago pastors were slightly overweight and wore outmoded suits every day of the week. Now they have charge accounts at Buckle.

When Rick Warren's *Purpose-Driven* model was touted as the new way of doing church and everyone kept admiring Saddleback Church, it was funny to see pastors around the world start wearing Hawaiian shirts like the ones Rick Warren always wears.

Petty.

All based on insecurity.

How often does our insecurity cause us to look at others and start comparing ourselves to them in little ways?

And those little ways—those petty ways—eat at us every day.

"Are the clothes I'm wearing good enough?"

"Is the car I drive OK?"

"Am I as pretty as she is?"

"Does my body look like hers?"

"Can I accomplish what that guy can accomplish?"

"Am I a faster runner?"

These petty comparisons grind on us every day. They keep our minds focused on why we're not good enough.

And if others are your rivals, then how can you really love them? How can you cheer on the best in others when all you really want is to be better than them? Or how can you care about others when you spend all your time just trying to be like them and get what they have?

In that paradigm either you *are* better than them and

build your memorial of pride even bigger, or you're *not* as good as them and your ego comes crashing down.

Petty.

And then it leads to bigger areas of comparison.

Just like what happened with Peter and John.

I know how this can be.

When we started Elevation Church in Utah in 2004, I was very aware of all the new churches gaining traction in the church-planting world. If a new church was doing a better job of reaching people and was growing faster than we were, I didn't rejoice with them. I got really depressed.

I'll be completely honest. When we started Elevation Church, we did a ton of research on the name "Elevation Church." We could find only one other church using that name, and it was located in Castle Rock, Colorado. They were a small, upstart church like we were.

We started the church.

We named it Elevation Church.

And when we went to secure all of our web stuff about ten months into the life of the church, we found out another church in North Carolina had just started with the name Elevation Church too.

So I kept my eyes on both the Colorado Elevation Church and the North Carolina Elevation Church.

The Colorado church dwindled and eventually closed its doors.

And I felt like I had accomplished something.

I felt like a success.

How messed up is that? I felt like a success because a church similar to ours in belief and practice had failed. I felt somehow better than them because we hadn't failed and they had.

On the other hand, the North Carolina church grew like a tick. It was being featured in magazines and touted as one of the fastest-growing churches in the United States.

Everyone seemed to know about them.

And it depressed me.

I felt like a failure any time I heard about this North Carolina Elevation Church. I cringed when asked if our Elevation Church was connected to theirs.

How messed up is that? My feelings of being a failure were attached to another church doing a great job of teaching others about Jesus. I was depressed about that.

The success of someone else had become my . . . failure?

Somehow the success of other Jesus communities was destroying my happiness.

Why?

Because of comparisons.

Insecurity does that.

It sabotages the happiness we have in ourselves, and it sabotages the relationship we have with others.

The apostle Paul tried to explain the love Jesus spoke about as it is extended to others. He wrote in his letter to the followers of Jesus who lived in Rome, "Rejoice with those who rejoice, weep with those who weep. Live in harmony with one another" (Rom. 12:15–16).

How could I ever weep with the Elevation Church in Colorado when their doors closed when I was touting myself as triumphant? How could I ever rejoice with the Elevation Church in North Carolina when I was depressed because of their success? There is no way I could love either one of those Jesus communities in a healthy way when I was playing the comparison game.

THE COMPARISON TRAP

If you're constantly trying to measure yourself against those around you, you're either going to dislike those who get more than you or exalt yourself over those you feel you have defeated in your measuring game.

Either one is lethal.

That isn't what God designed for your life.

Let's be honest. How often do we let our measuring game sabotage what God has for our lives?

"What about this man?"

"What does he get?"

"Is it better than what I get?"

> Jesus said to him, "If it is my will that he remain until I come, what is that to you? You follow me!"
>
> —JOHN 21:22

Jesus looks Peter in the face and says, "This isn't about you. This is about what *I* want. This is *My* will being done. Stop comparing yourself to John. I just want you to follow what *I* give you."

We have insecurities, but we have to stop comparing ourselves to others.

Oh, but it is so hard.

I know.

Especially when the marketing we see in advertisements uses this sabotaging compulsion to compare to try to sell us products.

"People who own this type of car are happy. Don't you want to be happy like this guy?"

"If you drink this beer, then you will be very interesting. Don't you want to be interesting like this guy?"

Marketers don't even realize they play this card so much because it comes out so naturally in all of us.

And this has been a problem since the beginning of human history. Adam and Eve, the first man and woman, have two sons, Cain and Abel. Both sons give offerings to God, but Abel's is more of a sacrifice than Cain's leftovers, and God gives favor and blessing to Abel for his.

Cain sees this and becomes very jealous.

So God speaks to Cain and asks him, "Why are you angry, and why has your face fallen? If you do well, will you not be accepted?" (Gen. 4:6–7).

Basically God is saying that Cain shouldn't get angry by looking at his brother's favor.

But Cain's anger.

Comparison.

Jealousy.

It all turns against Abel.

And one day Cain kills Abel.

Now Abel is dead, and Cain gets cursed by God.

And all along the problem wasn't Abel.

Cain's life is sabotaged by insecurity.

GETTING OUR FOCUS STRAIGHT

Peter's life could have been sabotaged, just like Cain's, but Jesus sets him straight.

"What is that to you?"

And really, that's a question for us.

It's a question for you.

"What is that to you?"

Every time you compare yourself to someone else, you let your insecurities steal the joy of life.

One word of caution here. Don't confuse the positive examples in your life to the unhealthy comparisons you make. Here is what I mean. If you completely stop caring about anyone and everyone around you, you will turn into what psychologists call an antisocial psychopath. These are the people who live in worlds in their own minds, where social interactions are based only on what they want to do and no one else matters.

This is not what I am getting at here. We learn appropriate social interactions and behavior by seeing others give us positive examples.

And Jesus is the ultimate positive example of what living is like.

Beyond His ultimate example we have positive examples around us all the time of what life is truly like when we walk with God. They teach us how to have healthy relationships and how to love ourselves without being self-centered.

It's good to take the feedback we encounter from those around us in order to calibrate our daily living. It's unhealthy to live completely outside of feedback, just as it's unhealthy to compare ourselves to others to decide if they are better, we are worse, we are better, or they are worse.

Stop comparing yourself to others.

These comparisons are a by-product of your insecurities, and they will only lead you to depression, sadness, and disconnected living.

You will separate yourself from others.

You will separate yourself from God.

Take the words of Jesus to heart when it comes to comparisons.

Allow yourself to be asked the question:

"What is that to you?"

Chapter 4

FEAR OF FAIR

You'll always win the gold medal in
this: Be who God made you to be.[1]
—RICK WARREN

During the 2012 Olympics, one story never reported on prime-time television to the American people came from the women's fencing competition.

During the semifinal women's fencing epee match, featuring Britta Heidemann of Germany and Shin A Lam of South Korea, Lam was in the lead with one second left on the clock. To make it to the gold medal match, Lam had to withstand being touched in that last second.

The referee signaled to restart the match, but the clock never got restarted. Britta Heidemann was given more than one second to make a touch on Lam. Heidemann was successful and then declared the winner.

The South Korean team was outraged and immediately appealed the decision.

Lam sat down on the playing surface to express she did not agree with the judges' decision. She sat, tears falling, for more than thirty minutes before her appeal was denied. In defiance of the decision, Lam refused to leave her sitting position on the playing surface and was eventually escorted out by security.

An emotionally distraught Lam was sent to the bronze medal match and lost.

One second from fencing for gold and then—nothing.

Sometime after the women's fencing incident took place, it was revealed that the timekeeper who failed to start the clock when the referee signaled the restart of the match was a fifteen-year-old volunteer.

Shin A Lam's loss of a chance at the gold medal was the result of a fifteen-year-old volunteer not hitting *start* on a clock and the appeals committee not accepting this as a reason to advance Lam to the gold match.[2]

One second.

A fifteen-year-old volunteer.

It wasn't fair.

THE BLAME GAME

All of us want to succeed in life.

Success is something we all strive for and want. Regardless of the sphere of life—school, sports, business, family, relationships—we all want to achieve it. And when we don't find success in an area of life, our first destination is blame. We start blaming someone or something else for why we didn't succeed.

We start to question if we were given a fair shot.

Did God give us a fair shot at success?

Did others treat us fairly?

Were the circumstances the same for us as it was for others who were successful?

Our insecurity keeps us in the comparison game. And beyond petty comparisons we question the fairness of life.

Was this fair?

If we're not careful, asking the fairness question can destroy the relationships around us.

We'll blame others.

We'll want what they have.

We'll start to desire a life somewhere over the rainbow—a fantasy that is a better existence—and we'll never really live in our now.

JACOB AND LABAN: FINGERS POINTED IN BOTH DIRECTIONS

Remember Jacob.

After he built the memorial to commemorate his bargain with God, he made his way to his uncle Laban's house.

His uncle had two daughters, and Jacob was attracted to the younger daughter, Rachel.

Laban wanted Jacob to work for him and sought to come up with a fair compensation for Jacob's work. Jacob, not having anything to give for a woman's hand in marriage, asked to marry Rachel in exchange for seven years of labor.

An agreement was made. Jacob worked seven years, and at the end of those seven years he expected to marry Rachel.

Now the story gets really weird.

A wedding takes place.

Jacob goes into the tent with his new wife and consummates the marriage.

In the morning he realizes it wasn't Rachel whom he married and slept with. It was Rachel's older sister, Leah!

I'm not exactly sure how Jacob missed that. Maybe there was a lot of drinking at the wedding or he didn't notice Rachel in the crowd at the wedding or he didn't realize Rachel's sister, Leah, wasn't there. Jacob seems like a smarter man than this story paints him to be. I'm still baffled at him missing this one.

In any case, he runs to his uncle and demands to know why Laban did this to him.

Not fair!

Not what they agreed to!

Laban explains that it would be inappropriate in their culture for the younger sister to marry before the older sister. He tells Jacob that if he finishes out the traditional festivities of the marriage week with Leah, then he will give Rachel to Jacob as his next wife.

But in order to be fair, Laban says, Jacob will have to work another seven years to pay for Rachel's hand in marriage.

Jacob agrees. He marries Rachel the following week and works another seven years for his uncle to complete his side of the agreement.

Then, after fourteen years of working for his uncle, Jacob asks to leave with his four wives (he had married both of his wives' servants by this time) and his twelve children. Laban pleads with Jacob to stay and continue working for him.

They agree upon a wage: Jacob will take all the speckled, spotted, and black sheep, as well as all the speckled and spotted goats. But before Jacob could separate out his wages from the rest of the flock, Laban has removed all the sheep and goats that are supposed to go to Jacob, sending them off with his sons on a three-day journey from where Jacob is.

Not fair.

But Jacob doesn't care.

He's back to his crafty, sly, and manipulative ways.

He figures out a way to breed sheep and goats so they're born with speckles and spots. And he applies this method of breeding to the strongest members of the flocks.

Leaving Laban the feeble and weak.

Laban's sons hear how rich and successful Jacob is becoming. And they, being the ones who are meant to inherit all that is their father's, become very angry and upset. "Not fair that Jacob is taking away our inheritance!" they cry.

Jacob realizes his welcome has run out.

He takes off with his wives, kids, servants, camels, donkeys, sheep, and goats and heads back to his homeland. He abandons his home and his uncle Laban without telling him he's leaving.

It doesn't take long for word to reach Laban that

Jacob has left with Laban's daughters and grandchildren. And so Laban, along with his kinsmen, takes to tracking down Jacob.

It takes seven days for them to catch up to Jacob.

You can imagine the scene when they finally catch him.

Jacob: "You said Rachel; I got Leah."

Labab: "Yeah, well, I trusted you with my goats and grandkids."

A simple family business plan gone awry.

Tit for tat.

Everyone's sense of fairness pushed to the limit.

Did Jacob treat Laban fairly? No. He manipulated his payment by breeding the flocks to his benefit. He lied to Laban, saying he wouldn't run off with his daughters and grandchildren, and then he ran off anyway.

Did Laban treat Jacob fairly? No. He hid Jacob's initial payment of speckled and spotted livestock. He tricked Jacob into working seven years for marriage to a daughter Jacob didn't want.

Here they were, at this intersection of relational strife, looking at each other in accusation, each treated unfairly by the other.

What's more, Laban's sons don't feel like they are being treated fairly.

And Laban's daughters don't feel like they are being treated fairly either.

While she isn't given a starring role in the biblical

narrative, think of how Leah must have felt being traded as a commodity to a man who didn't want her in the first place.

This is what the comparison game does.

It breaks down relationships.

It paints pictures of mistrust and blame.

Fairness means everyone begins on an equal playing field with no advantages—same starting point and same rewards as the others who do what we did or are doing or are given what we were promised or expected.

Fairness means we are not manipulated or cheated along the path to achieving our goals.

This sense of fairness attacks Jacob and Laban, who were both tricksters. (Perhaps it's genetic?) Each man tastes his own medicine, and it breaks down all their relationships.

Really picture this.

It's a dead ringer for a *Jerry Springer* episode, for sure.

A guy marries his two cousins and their two servants, has twelve kids, and his uncle and brothers-in-law and cousins chase him into the middle of nowhere because everyone's upset with everyone else.

You know what happens next.

They come to an agreement.

I wouldn't call what happens a complete reconciliation, but they do reach an agreement.

They agree to walk away from each other.

In other words, they agree to never meet up again and to stay away from each other.

And then they build a memorial to remember their agreement.

Just like Jacob did before, he puts a rock vertically in the ground. And next to his vertical rock memorial, he instructs his family to pile up a heap of other rocks. They call this memorial "Heap of Witnesses." The heap of rocks serves as a representation of all those who witnessed the agreement made between Jacob and Laban.

Not only do they build the memorial to remember their agreement, but they also build it to act as a guidepost geographically, indicating where Jacob's kinsmen and Laban's kinsmen would not pass to the other side. It's an indicator for how they would stay separated from each other.

They agree to disagree.

They agree to keep away.

They walk away in distrust, but also agreeing to do no more harm.

And the way they will do no harm is to commit to not contact each other.

FAIRNESS DRIVES A WEDGE

Separation is the result of the fairness game.

When our insecurities keep us centered on ourselves, disliking our lives, comparing ourselves to others, asking if things are fair, we sabotage the relationships closest to us.

So, let's recap.

You have insecurities.

This isn't about you.

Stop comparing yourself to others.

And stop thinking this world is fair.

Being the oldest child in my dad's family and being the oldest child in my mom's family had its advantages and disadvantages.

There are eight years separating me from my next oldest sibling in my dad's family. Eleven years separating me from the next. And sixteen years separating me from the youngest.

The age difference growing up was vast.

And since my dad was so young when he had me, he wasn't in the prime income-earning stage of his life when I was at the height of my dependence on him.

If I wanted a car, I had to buy it.

Which I did.

If I wanted a pager (there were no cell phones when I was in high school!), I had to buy it.

Which I did.

If I wanted to go to the movies or go on a date, I had to pay for it.

Which I did.

If I wanted to go to college, I had to worry about scholarships and finances.

Which I did.

Now, my brother and sisters had a different experience growing up.

If they wanted a car, my dad bought them one.

If they wanted a cell phone, my dad paid for theirs.

If they wanted to go to the movies, they just had to ask.

(I am, of course, overdramatizing this for effect.)

Not fair.

I wondered, "Why do they get all this stuff for free while I had to work my butt off for it?"

There were times when I felt a resentment rise up inside of me, when I heard of the new cars, the college expenses, and the cell phones my father bought for them.

It started to drive a wedge into my relationships with all of them.

I didn't want to be around my dad anymore because I felt angry he wasn't being fair.

I didn't want to be around my siblings because I was jealous.

Any parent will tell you there's no way you can treat your children with absolute fairness. There are just too many variables playing into the decisions you make with each one. Outside forces that sometimes dictate your actions, and each child is their own person with their own actions and reactions too.

One of my dear friends, Jim, tells me that each one of his kids, when asked who they think is the favorite child in the family, will name a different kid. He says he knows everything will not be completely fair, but he feels he has done his part as a parent when he hears that response from his children.

I realize, now that I'm a lot older and have had time to work through my insecurities, that my siblings have different perspectives on all those events than I did.

Who got to stay out later?

I did.

Who got to do almost anything he wanted?

I did.

Who got more freedom from the rules?

I did.

My siblings measured other areas of their lives with me in terms of fairness, and their wedges, coupled with my wedge, started to divide us.

All over the idea of fairness.

It's a game, really.

This fairness game comes down to an insecurity issue inside us.

And it sabotages relationships.

It turns out everyone's parents were correct.

Life really isn't fair.

Gold medal moments are lost by timekeeper errors. We're swindled out of wages by family members. Our parents give more to one child than another. People are greedy and will do anything to get more. Life is not fair by our perspective.

THE FIRST WILL BE LAST

In the Book of Matthew we find a story written about Jesus and fairness.

Peter comes up to Jesus and says, "See, we have left everything and followed you. What then will we have?" (Matt. 19:27).

The disciples gave up their lives to follow after Jesus. Before they met Him, they were living such different lives. We hear how they were fishermen or tax collectors and walked away from those lives so they could learn from Jesus. I'm sure they gave up more than professions to follow after Jesus. They probably gave up lots of relational connections and their standing within their communities too.

Peter isn't just telling Jesus something He would already know—that they gave up everything to follow Him. Peter is ultimately asking, "So what's in this for those of us who really follow You? What's in it for me? What is my service worth? I can sever a human ear from its skull—is that a valuable skill? What do I get?"

And here's how Jesus responds:

> Jesus said to them, "Truly, I say to you, in the new world, when the Son of Man will sit on his glorious throne, you who have followed me will also sit on twelve thrones, judging the twelve tribes of Israel. And everyone who has left houses or brothers or sisters or father or mother or children or lands, for my name's sake, will receive a hundredfold and will inherit eternal life."
>
> —MATTHEW 19:28–29

Jesus tells Peter not to worry about what he will get. He will get eternal life with Jesus, and he's also been chosen as a leader among the Jews of those who follow after Jesus.

Now look at the next thing Jesus says:

> But many who are first will be last, and the last first.
>
> —MATTHEW 19:30

Jesus is trying to tell Peter that many people who start following Jesus at the beginning are going to feel as if they are last, and many who start following Jesus last are going to feel as if they are first.

Peter is asking Jesus about fairness, and Jesus lets him know they're all getting what they were promised. But if they base their willingness to follow Jesus on their feelings, no one is going to feel as if any of this is fair.

What?

You see, we usually don't cry unfair when a time-keeper's mistake gets us *into* the gold medal match, but we cry unfair if that same mistake *keeps* us from getting a chance at the medal.

Jesus used lots of stories to explain God's perspective versus our perspective. And that is exactly what Jesus did next after answering Peter's question—He broke out into story.

> For the kingdom of heaven is like a master of
> a house who went out early in the morning to
> hire laborers for his vineyard. After agreeing
> with the laborers for a denarius a day, he sent
> them into his vineyard.
>
> —MATTHEW 20:1–2

It was pretty typical of this time period to go and find day laborers for agricultural work.

Make note that the master in Jesus's story agrees to pay these day laborers a denarius *early* in the morning for the work they will do all day. It's early when he hires them. And it's a denarius that he promises them—which would have been bare minimum pay to take care of a family during this time period.

Then the story continues:

> And going out about the third hour he saw
> others standing idle in the marketplace, and
> to them he said, "You go into the vineyard too,

and whatever is right I will give you." So they
went.

—MATTHEW 20:3–5

Mid-morning this master goes out and sees there are
other day laborers not working. Maybe he felt bad they
weren't working to provide for their families. Whatever
his reason the master asks them to work for him for
the day.

And then:

> Going out again about the sixth hour and the
> ninth hour, he did the same.
> —MATTHEW 20:5

Two more times the master goes out and finds poten-
tial laborers who are not working and offers them work.
Finally:

> And about the eleventh hour he went out and
> found others standing. And he said to them,
> "Why do you stand here idle all day?" They
> said to him, "Because no one has hired us." He
> said to them, "You go into the vineyard too."
> —MATTHEW 20:6–7

This part of Jesus's story really clues us into the spec-
ulation we might have had earlier in the story. Why
would the master keep going out to get more laborers?
It appears he is really concerned with making sure
no one is going to go without. This benevolent master

finds work so these simple laborers can take care of themselves and their families.

Now here is where it gets really unfair:

> And when evening came, the owner of the vineyard said to his foreman, "Call the laborers and pay them their wages, beginning with the last, up to the first."
>
> —MATTHEW 20:8

It's a little interesting that the master would want those who were hired last to be paid first, but this is Jesus's point. Let's read on:

> And when those hired about the eleventh hour came, each of them received a denarius. Now when those hired first came, they thought they would receive more, but each of them also received a denarius. And on receiving it they grumbled at the master of the house, saying, "These last worked only one hour, and you have made them equal to us who have borne the burden of the day and the scorching heat."
>
> —MATTHEW 20:9–12

Plainly put, this isn't fair.

Let's be honest—we would be very upset if we were in their shoes.

At least, I would.

And I'm pretty sure you would too.

My response would be the same as theirs but with

different words: "My time is worth more! I'm worth more! This isn't fair!"

> But he [the master] replied to one of them, "Friend, I am doing you no wrong. Did you not agree with me for a denarius?"
>
> —MATTHEW 20:13

Think back to the beginning of the story Jesus told.

Those who were hired early in the morning would have been so happy to be chosen as workers for the day. They got a job! They were going to be able to provide for their families.

But the end of the story is a little different.

The workers who went without getting hired all day had probably settled into the fact that even though they'd been hired at the eleventh hour, only able to work one hour that day, the day as a whole was a bust, and they hadn't made enough money to care for their families that day. When they stood in line to get their pay for their hour of work and saw how much it was, their excitement and happiness would have been the same as those back in the early morning—they were going to be able to provide for their families!

The story kind of echoes Jesus's words to Peter earlier:

> But many who are first will be last, and the last first.
>
> —MATTHEW 19:30

If there were no eleventh-hour employees, no one would have grumbled about his pay at the end of the day. But when they started to compare themselves to one another, all their insecurities started to boil out. Suddenly their relationship with the master is damaged and their resentment toward other employees erupts.

Jesus ends His story by taking us back to the concept that this is about God and His plan—His purpose in the world—not ours:

> Take what belongs to you and go. I choose to give to this last worker as I give to you. Am I not allowed to do what I choose with what belongs to me? Or do you begrudge my generosity?
>
> —MATTHEW 20:14–15

Sometimes the last are going to feel as if they are first.

Sometimes the first are going to feel as if they are last.

Because in the eternal perspective of God there are no positions.

No one is ahead of the other.

No one needs to worry about what they have been given or not given.

No one needs to worry about what others have received.

No one needs to compare.

No one needs to let their security be based on what they have.

Your worth and security are not based on a scale that is trying to balance out the world. And if you let your worth and security start playing the fairness game, you will destroy the relationships around you. You will sabotage what Jesus said was truly living *life*: loving others, loving God, and loving ourselves.

IT'S ABOUT RELATIONSHIPS

I've never hidden the fact that I've spent time seeing a counselor. He's a godly man who has helped me think through so many areas of life, especially relationships. And one of the things he has most helped me understand is that these unhealthy patterns of living we've been talking about create vicious cycles that eat away at our relationships.

The lie that gets implanted in our head is that eventually things will work themselves out. It's a lie because these unhealthy patterns just lead us further and further down a path of insecurity, which leads to decayed relationships, which leads to selfish living, which leads to not trusting others, which leads to not trusting God.

See?

It's a vicious cycle.

Maybe you've seen these patterns in your life.

You don't trust people.

You're nervous about how others view you or what they'll think about you.

You stay away from them.

You don't trust God.

You think He doesn't love you as He does others.

You stay away from Him and anything that has to do with Him.

You don't trust yourself either.

You might be to blame for all those failed relationships.

It's too hard to figure it all out now, so why bother?

You just keep hurting yourself.

You close yourself off from trying to heal.

And if you let it, the sabotage cycle just keeps going.

Chapter 5

NO ADDITIVES ALLOWED

I don't need the fillers, additives, excessive amounts of sugars, fats, salts, and other measures taken to taint the natural goodness of real food.[1]
—MARK HYMAN, MD

'VE NOT EXPERIENCED too many bucket list moments, but one of those moments happened last year.

I had the opportunity—not planned, but by happenstance—to attend one of the top restaurants in the United States, which also happened to be ranked among the top fifty restaurants in the world.

I'm not talking about going onto the Internet and looking up the top-reviewed restaurants in a city or seeing what the local critics say about the best places to eat. I'm talking about a premier restaurant, with an eight-month wait list and a world-renowned chef.

Thanks to a great friend of mine, Doug, who happens to know the brother of the chef, we ended up with reservations to that top restaurant, just because we happened to be in the area.

No eight-month wait.

We just slipped right in.

So here we were, not prepared to go to a restaurant of this magnitude, walking in with our jeans and the only collared shirts we happened to have in our luggage for the trip. We stuck out like a sore thumb.

It probably didn't help that we were the only guests outside taking pictures of ourselves next to the sign and the building, bubbling with excitement that we were going to eat at a place that was way out of our league.

Our party, which included Doug, myself, and two

pastor friends who were traveling with us, were seated after a very short wait. The ambiance was what I had pictured in my mind based on all the television shows and movies I had seen with amazing restaurants in them.

But what I wasn't prepared for was the level of service.

Nor was I prepared for the food.

Our menus came, and when we opened them up, we had one option on the left page and one option on the right page.

Two options.

A ten-course meal, all spelled out.

Or a twelve-course meal, chef's choice.

When were we ever going to experience something like this again? We picked the chef's choice.

I felt caught up in a movie after we made that decision, because the service of the place came alive. I am pretty sure they were all singing "Be Our Guest" from the *Beauty and the Beast* Disney animated film, because their service matched the tune.

We didn't have one waiter, like in most restaurants. We had the whole service staff serving us.

If I dropped a crumb, it was scrapped off the linen with a special knife.

If I got up to go to the restroom, my napkin was replaced with a new, freshly folded one.

If a new course was coming, our silverware was

completely replaced with new, clean silverware that we would use for that course. (This happened twelve times!)

While in conversation with each other, we would look down and realize that new food had been set down for us to enjoy. It was like magic.

And when the wait staff would arrive with each course, four people would bring the four plates for our table, and it was synchronized so that two plates would be placed in front of us and then the next two plates.

The service was an art form!

And the food...how do I even begin to tell you about the food?

Reading about the restaurant online and the brief conversation I had with the maître d' told me everything we were going to eat was grown from a garden on-site and that the chef owned all of the animals used to produce the other ingredients.

This was going to be different than Applebee's for sure.

From the moment I took a bite of the first appetizer jelly square that was laid in front of me, I knew I was in for something I had never experienced before. Each bite after that one brought with it new flavors I had tasted before, but never in the way I was tasting them in that moment. At times I stopped paying attention to the announcement of what we were eating, because

I knew it would taste nothing like what I had tasted before when eating the same food.

Take the butter, for instance.

Butter.

Of all things, the butter.

It was delivered to us on a rock slate, and it was like cutting into a soft cheese. The flavor was more than that creamy dairy taste we're all used to. It was creamy, but there was a salty, seasoned taste to it too that we all sat and tried to pinpoint.

What was in the butter?

The maître d' came over to check on us frequently, maybe because we were there by invitation of the chef's brother or maybe because we looked like four men who were homeless and eating food for the first time. We were loud, laughing, and out of our element. When he came over to us, our first request was, "Can we get more butter? We're sure you get that request a lot, but this is the best butter we have ever tasted."

He looked around the restaurant, hushing us with a secretive look on his face. "Shhhh," he said. "Not everyone gets the butter."

"Not everyone gets the butter?"

"No. Tonight, only you guys get the butter, and the number-one chef in all of Japan is visiting us, and his party gets the butter too." He pointed across the restaurant to a two-table party.

"Well, why is this butter so special—what do they put in it?" we asked.

"The chef lives in Santa Cruz. He loves to kayak, so he takes a one-gallon bucket and kayaks out into the ocean until he hits the buoy at mile-marker one. Then he fills his bucket up with saltwater and kayaks back to shore. He takes that bucket of saltwater and dries it out to produce his own salt. He then goes and milks his own cow. They take the milk from that cow and churn it by hand. It takes five hours. The chef adds the salt he dried out from the ocean to it, and then they churn it some more. It takes five hours to produce the seven sticks of butter we're using tonight. Nothing else is added."

We all sat there in amazement.

Nothing else added.

This butter was as fresh as you could get. Nothing processed in a factory or preservatives added to give it shelf life.

It was the definition of fresh.

The chef eventually came out to say hi to us, and we even got a backstage pass to view the kitchen. The only thing I could come up with to say was, "The butter was amazing!"

When we finished our four-hour, twelve-course meal—I will not tell you how much it cost—I sat there amazed at the tastes I had experienced that day. Everything I ate was as fresh as that butter.

In the daze of the moment I'm not sure who said it in our group, but one of us said, "I didn't know food was suppose to taste like that."

Nothing added.

Fresh.

The best food I have ever eaten has been food that was fresh. When my wife and I were in Hawaii, just driving down a winding road, exploring the island of Maui, we came upon a fisherman catching fish off the side of the island. She was cutting up the fish right there and throwing them on a grill as fast she could. I don't think I saw her season them at all, but she was making kabobs for anyone willing to throw some money her way. To this day it was the best fish I have ever eaten.

The mangoes I picked off the trees in Cambodia—best mangoes I have ever eaten.

The plums off my grandfather's trees—best plums I have ever eaten.

The peaches off my mother-in-law's trees—best peaches I have ever eaten.

There's something about food that is fresh, presented just as it was designed to be: unaltered, no additives, no preservatives, unprocessed.

THE NOTHING-ADDED LIFE

There's something about life when it's lived this way too: unaltered, with no additives.

Insecurities, as we learned in chapter 1, create defense mechanisms—additives—to real, unadulterated living. These defense mechanisms protect us from the feelings of mistrust, hurt, or lack of safety. But they also keep us in a vicious cycle of disconnection from who we really are and from others. Primarily they disconnect us from our Creator, God.

Let me show you what I'm talking about.

The apostle Paul wrote a letter to the followers of Jesus who were living in Galatia. This letter is, by far, my favorite of the New Testament letters, primarily because Paul summarizes what this whole living-for-God-and-following-Jesus thing is all about.

At the beginning of Galatians 5 Paul summarizes a lot of what he has been talking about in the letter so far and what he wants others to know about Jesus. He says:

> For freedom Christ has set us free; stand firm therefore, and do not submit again to a yoke of slavery.
>
> —GALATIANS 5:1

Here's what I want you to know. There is a way of life that is freedom for our soul, our very being, our everything. It is the driving force behind everything we do.

We want freedom from pain.

From want.

From the weight of the world.

From being bound.

From inner turmoil.

From chaos.

From the things that haunt us.

From our failures.

From the things that gnaw inside of us.

From _____. (You fill in the blank.)

You and I know that what we really have been searching for all this time is freedom. *Freedom*—that absolutely unaltered life of peace, safety, and security. And this freedom we are searching for is the very reason Jesus came and died on the cross for us. He is the way to this freedom, and He is the one who provides it.

The freedom we yearn for is discovered from living in Christ.

So here is where this gets all messy. Please have faith and stay with me in this.

In order for you to experience the life in Christ you were meant to experience—the life where your insecurities are completely abolished—it's going to take some work.

Here's one way to put it. It's going to take a one-mile row out to mile-marker one in the middle of the ocean, then a return row with a one-gallon bucket of saltwater in tow, then a cow getting milked for hours, then milk getting churned for hours, then adding salt and doing more churning.

In other words, this process of being set free from our insecurities and finding real life in Christ won't happen overnight, and it won't happen without some hard work and the overcoming of obstacles.

It isn't easy.

In fact, I'm going to say a hard thing here. (And I hope you don't throw this book across the room when you read it. Trust me—it won't be worth the tort lawsuit you'd be up against if you hit someone when you throw it.)

When it comes down to it, you have a choice: the freedom God offers or the cycle of slavery you've been living in.

When we feel unsafe and our insecurities about life and ourselves are exposed, we start doing everything we can to obtain that feeling of safety and freedom again. In fact, some of us have no clue what it even feels like to have safety, peace, and freedom. We might have tasted something called butter before, but once we know what real butter tastes like, we'll be able to taste the mechanized process behind all the other regular sticks of butter we ever taste again. That is what defense mechanisms become for us: cheap imitations of safety, peace, and freedom.

Jacob wanted freedom from being stuck as the second-born, living in the shadow of Esau, his miracle father, Isaac, and his patriarch grandfather, Abraham.

John wanted freedom from not being the oldest, boldest disciple.

Peter wanted freedom from not measuring up and from failing when called upon.

I wanted freedom from feeling unwanted and unaccepted.

We all want freedom.

And a lack of safety pushes us to add things into our lives that rip away at the fabric of experiencing the real life we are meant to live with the one who made life in the first place

This is what Paul is talking about in chapter 5 of Galatians. He talks about how religious people add rules and regulations with the hope that those rules will bring them ultimate freedom and closer to God. But Paul is trying to tell them they've never tasted butter like the kind that Christ offers before. Only Jesus can give this butter to you, and nothing—no process or security system—will bring true freedom like what's found in Christ's offering to you.

But we erect memorials of pride—a defense mechanism—to maybe quench the longing for freedom.

We compare ourselves to others—a defense mechanism—to maybe quench the longing for freedom.

We play the fair game with others—a defense

mechanism—to maybe quench the longing for freedom.

This cycle is an absolute war raging inside us.

This war is between our humanity—our flesh, as Paul puts it—and the way God created things to work, or the spirit of God.

Flesh versus spirit.

A tale as old as time.

Here is how Paul described this war:

> But I say, walk by the Spirit, and you will not gratify the desires of the flesh. For the desires of the flesh are against the Spirit, and the desires of the Spirit are against the flesh, for these are opposed to each other, to keep you from doing the things you want to do.
> —GALATIANS 5:16–17

Paul urges us to long for the way God created things to be and to not fall victim to the sabotage of our desires, which try to get us to find that freedom we've always wanted in roundabout, unhealthy ways.

Your processed way and God's natural and arduous ways don't mix.

Let me put it, again, bluntly. Your subconscious conscious patterns of life, your defense mechanisms, your insecurities, your internal desires for freedom, your attempts at manufacturing freedom…all of these things? They don't give you an ounce of freedom.

Only God can give you freedom.

And this, my friends, is why insecurity separates us from God.

It leads us to blame God for our lack of safety, security, and peace. We think God messed up somehow. And so we try to fix things only God can fix.

Although we want freedom, we perpetually buy into this lie that says God's mistakes are fixable by our desires and pursuits and that the world has the answer.

But Paul says this:

> If you are led by the Spirit, you are not under the law.
>
> —GALATIANS 5:18

Here Paul is saying that if you're following after Jesus and want to live for God, then your freedom cannot be found in man-made ways.

On the other hand Paul says:

> Now the works of the flesh are evident.
>
> —GALATIANS 5:19

So Paul explains to us what happens when, consciously or subconsciously, we try to find freedom on our own. For the next three verses he rolls out a laundry list of desires we give into to try to find that freedom and medicate the insecurities inside of us. It's not an exhaustive list he gives us, by any means, but a glimpse at the war raging inside.

He rolls out the laundry list as follows:

> Sexual immorality, impurity, sensuality, idolatry, sorcery, enmity, strife, jealousy, fits of anger, rivalries, dissensions, divisions, envy, drunkenness, orgies, and things like these.
> —GALATIANS 5:19–21

Maybe a laundry list is a bad way to describe this list to gain an understanding of what Paul is trying to reveal to us. Think about this list as a ladder.

We'll start at the bottom rung of the ladder and work our way up.

And by the way, no one starts at the top of the ladder.

Each rung leads to the next rung.

Let's walk up this ladder together.

SEXUAL IMMORALITY

The Greek word Paul uses here for "sexual immorality," *porneia*, is where we get our English word "porn"—just a little FYI. But don't put a modern-day American definition on this word, because the original readers of this letter would have understood Paul to be talking about having sex with someone who is not your spouse. This would apply to those who were married, as well as those who were not yet married. If you weren't married, this would mean having sex with anyone, since you didn't have a spouse yet.

Now God created sex.

It wasn't an accident.

He didn't create man and woman, walk away one day, and then come back the next to find them doing something He didn't expect to happen. God created the physiology of our bodies to have sex. It was an act created for both the procreation of humanity and the enjoyment of each other. God designed it this way.

Now God also created sex to be a mutually beneficial and intimate experience between two people. The souls of two people mingle through sex, and it transcends mere physical actions.

How do I know this? When someone is abused sexually or raped, are they healed once their physical body heals?

Of course not.

This is bigger than something physical.

It is emotional.

It is spiritual.

It affects the totality of who we are, and when we engage in sex, we are giving the totality of who we are to someone else. This is not a book about sex being only for marriage, but you can see why God would only intend for us to have sex within the confines of marriage when it is such an intimate and bonding experience.

God created sex as a physical and spiritual act to be done within the confines of a covenant that God called marriage. So when you go outside that covenant to mingle your body and soul with others, you are taking parts of them that don't belong to you, and you are giving them parts of yourself that don't belong to them.

God knows true freedom comes through living the way He designed things to be, and when we step out of that way of living, living instead by our own desires, thinking our freedom comes from quenching those desires, we only hurt ourselves more.

God is the one path to what life really is, what freedom really is, and when we choose to walk another path, we separate ourselves from Him.

There are many reasons we might dive into sexual immorality to try to obtain freedom from our insecurities. We may think that having sex with other people outside of marriage will bring us the acceptance we have so longed for—a freedom from being unaccepted. We may think that having sex with other people outside of marriage will bring us love we have so longed for—a freedom from being unloved. We may think it will bring us the achievement of some messed-up level of success—freedom from being a failure.

There are too many possibilities to list here.

When I was finishing up my bachelor's degree and started working on a master's degree at a seminary, I met another seminary student who came from a long line of pastors. His dad was a pastor, his grandfather was a pastor, and his brothers were pastors. He felt mounds of pressure to be a successful pastor. He found himself at seminary because he had been fired by two different churches and felt that maybe a seminary degree, which none of his pastoral family members ever achieved, would make him a success.

One day this young man came to me and another friend of ours to confess his failures. As he sat in front of us, staring at the floor, he opened up that he was having "sex talks" online with girls. He said he couldn't stop. It made him feel wanted and loved.

This young man was searching for freedom, and he had believed a lie that if he let his desires inside himself run the show, they would lead him to the freedom he so desperately was searching for.

It didn't though.

I watched as, years later, he found a girl he fell in love with, they began to talk marriage, and he told her about his "sex talk" problem. She was hurt, and it took a little while for them to work through the pain that was bringing into their relationship.

Do you really think sexual immorality brings any of us freedom?

Somehow we subconsciously—and maybe consciously—think it does, so we live it out, thinking we know better than God what will bring us freedom from our insecurities.

This is the bottom rung of the ladder, maybe because

the most natural desire inside of us is our sexual appetite. Psychologists have said for years that physical touch is one of the most basic needs we have, and it makes sense that we would use it in inappropriate ways to try to find the freedom we're searching for.

IMPURITY AND SENSUALITY

Some translations of the Bible use the word *debauchery* for the word *sensuality*. *Debauchery* is an ancient word, and I'm not sure of the last time you or I have heard someone use it in a legitimate sentence.

But Paul uses the two words *impurity* and *sensuality* to describe stuff that we just plain know is wrong, and no matter how hard we work at trying to stay away from those things, we still run to them to get them to bring us freedom.

Let me use this example. It's as if you know that drinking poison, even a little sip every day, will harm you. You lecture others about it and warn people to stay away from doing it, but when you feel the shackles of insecurity and you're searching for that feeling of freedom, you sip that poison.

For you, the poison might be drugs.

It might be an eating disorder.

It might be porn.

It might be the wrong relationships.

It might be anything you know is wrong, but it owns you.

Freedom doesn't come from being a slave to any-thing on this earth. It comes only from God. Your insecurities will not be fixed by an earthly master, but these things become our earthly masters when we've turned what we know is unhealthy into a habit—a habit we can't get out of.

One day a young adult from our church called to ask for help dealing with his problem of chronic mastur-bation. This conversation will always ring in my ears, because I remember him saying, "Every time I feel alone and unwanted, I go look at porn on the Internet and masturbate. I am so ashamed when I'm done—I'm the one teaching others not to do it, and here I am, unable to stop myself."

His habit had become his master. What he knew was evil owned him. He went to it for freedom from his loneliness, and it left him with shame. It cured nothing and gave him more chains.

What male hasn't turned to masturbation to try to cure the feeling of loneliness? Our bodies were made to connect with our spouses in a very physical way. And we can actually manipulate our bodies into thinking we did make that physical connection, thus giving our-selves the physical feeling of connection.

The problem, as every male knows, is that after we manipulate our bodies into thinking that connection actually took place, our spiritual and emotional states collide with reality. This is where the feelings of shame and guilt hit someone not more than a minute after that elation from the physical manipulation of connection transpired. That climax was meant to be shared with someone else. Absent of another, it leaves us no closer to freedom than when we first tried using masturbation to find it.

IDOLATRY AND WITCHCRAFT

Remembering that each word plays off the next, leads from one to the next like ladder rungs, you can see why Paul would go from debauchery to talking about idolatry and witchcraft—having a master that you don't want mastering you to having a master you chose to serve.

I mean, quite frankly, this can be the worship of any god or religion other than the God of the Bible. You think that that god will bring you freedom, but it doesn't.

Voodoo magic.

Witchcraft.

Spells.

Spirit worship.

The common response here is thinking this isn't happening in our American culture, or Western culture, like it happens in other countries. Guess again. As a pastor I heard the confessions of people relying on the demonic realm and witchcraft to get them through their days, spilling their own blood or others' blood to seal the spell that was cast.

The desire for freedom can lead you to some deep, dark areas.

And it can go beyond the folklore tales of peasants in a faraway land conjuring up spirits. It can be the ways we worship with our money and time—things we don't automatically classify as worship but is the same as any pagan religious act around the world.

While I was in Cambodia, I noticed that everyone had these little birdhouse-looking things on wooden beams outside their houses. I asked a person who lived in Cambodia what they were, and they explained that people worship the spirits around them and these little birdhouse things were the houses where the spirits would come take their offerings. At times I would see food or incense burning in these little houses. People believed that by spending money and time on these offerings, their futures could be changed by acts of the spirits.

Coming from the perspective of American culture, we might find that silly. But Cambodia doesn't have state-run lotteries. In our culture you find millions of people hoping their future will change based on the correctly numbered Ping-Pong balls blown up a chute. Which is more odd: hoping in birdhouse spirits or in fan-blown Ping-Pong balls?

We worship lots of things other than God.

STRIFE

Or, as other translations say, *hatred*.

Sometimes we think if we hate others or a certain someone, it will bring freedom from the pain they caused us or that something else caused us.

Sometimes it has nothing to do with being hurt but everything to do with control. If our rage can control those around us, we satisfy an inward desire that's looking to quench the lack of control we felt in our past or the insecurity we live with today.

Sometimes it has nothing to do with control or pain but everything to do with trying to feel less-than or not good enough. If we can hate others and make them less than us with our anger, we place ourselves above them, better than them.

Strife and hatred are defense mechanisms that we use, hoping they will free us from our insecurities.

But they are toxic to our relationships.

As a pastor I knew this girl who hated men. Absolutely couldn't stand any man. She had great relationships with women, and if you watched her interact with women, she was awesome. But her interactions with men, on the other hand? Terrible.

She worked at a restaurant, and I would watch her light up when talking to the women she served. But if a man came in to order something, she treated him with disrespect and disgust. It got so bad—she had enough complaints against her—that her job was on the line.

One day we were in a conversation, and she finally opened up to me. She shared that she didn't know how to talk to men because she hated them so much. I asked her why she hated them so much.

She looked up to the sky and then looked back at me. "Well, that is an easy answer—because my dad used to beat me and my mom."

"Do you think hating men heals that pain you have from your father?" I asked.

"No. But I know that's why I do it, and I don't know how to stop. It's ruining my life."

Hatred will consume you so that eventually you become the very thing you hate. I watched this young lady hate men, talk to them as if they were trash, and give them no respect, all because of her father. She didn't see she was becoming her father to these men. She was becoming the very thing she hated.

Hatred is like having a fire burning inside you. You start the fire because you're upset about something, but the only person who gets hurt is you. It will never bring you freedom or cure your insecurities.

JEALOUSY

Don't confuse the healthy jealousy for unhealthy jealousy here.

Healthy jealousy is the kind God has for you when you give your worship to something other than Him. Think about it like this. If your spouse fell in love with someone other than you and was giving all their time, emotions, admiration, respect, love, and affection to this other person, you would feel jealous. What is rightfully yours is being given to someone else. In the same way, you are God's and you belong to Him. When your affection is not directed at Him, He gets jealous. He wants what is rightfully His.

In this passage Paul isn't talking about the healthy kind of jealousy. He's talking about the unhealthy kind, where we're wanting something that isn't rightfully ours and despising anyone who has what we want.

Unhealthy jealousy keeps us playing the "fair" game we talked about in chapter 4.

Here, we don't rejoice with those who are rejoicing. We sit and want what they've been rewarded, wishing it was our life and hating them for their good fortune. Here, we don't mourn with those who are mourning. We rejoice, thinking they deserved what they got in life. We think their misfortune was destined and fair.

We want others to get what's due to them in life, and we think that if the scales of justice were completely in balance, then all would work out.

The problem with that is you.

If you got what you deserved, as far as punishment goes, it would be bad news.

Do you see the disconnect that exists here? We think if we get what they have or if things were fair, then we would have freedom. But all it brings is slavery to a constant battle with those around us and ourselves.

We're not happy with others, with ourselves, or with God.

Have you ever driven on the interstate and watched someone fly by you, speeding like a crazed lunatic? The first thought that runs through your head is, "Man, I hope a cop is up there to catch that maniac." But when it's you speeding down the road because you're late for work, your thought is, "Oh, Jesus, please don't let there be a cop on this interstate."

Jealousy is like drinking a poison to kill someone else, but it doesn't kill them. It only kills you. It leaves you thrashing inside for something to happen to someone else, but you are the only one ever affected.

FITS OF ANGER

Do you ever find yourself blowing up at the littlest of things? Confession time for me: I have grown some in this area, but it ignites in me enough to say that anger is something that subconsciously lives inside of me.

This could be about control.

This could be about not being able to grasp what we so desperately want—like a teakettle hitting its whistle, we could be so unhappy not having freedom that we explode when something reminds us we still haven't found it.

If things don't happen exactly as we want them to happen, we think the world needs to hear our disgust.

Could it be that we think our reaction will bring peace and freedom from something bigger inside of us?

Fits of anger are expressions of a raged war inside of us, but not actions to a solution. No amount of charged rage will bring goodness and contentment to our lives. Anger only leads to more anger, which leads to more anger, which destroys us. What amount of intensity that is directed at a situation to bring peace only leads us to more struggles.

Rivalries

This is what we talked about in chapter 3—we compare ourselves to everyone around us.

We build caste systems and hierarchies, thinking if we get to some level others have achieved, maybe we will gain some sense of freedom.

This isn't us versus the world.

There is no level to achieve.

There's nothing you can gain in this world that someone else has already gained that will bring you freedom.

As Paul says:

> Not that we dare to classify or compare ourselves with some of those who are commending themselves. But when they measure themselves by one another and compare themselves with one another, they are without understanding.
> —2 Corinthians 10:12

We don't need to compare ourselves to others. This is not about being better than others or playing some game to win.

Rivalries and comparisons will never bring us freedom. They'll just sweep us up into a never-ending cycle of needing to keep up and stay on top.

DISSENSIONS AND DIVISIONS

With dissensions and divisions we're forming teams and keeping score on purpose. This is like playing the comparison game, only amplified—creating one tribe in order to destroy another tribe.

Inside the human psyche we feel that if we have a group identity, our acceptance will be cured, our longing for worth will be quenched, and we'll have taken our rivalries to a more complex level.

This can happen if we have a team around us or a group we identify with. It can happen with political parties, race groups, activist groups, clubs, and social economic groups. It can happen outside a formal group and also with a few people.

I saw dissensions and divisions so many times as a pastor. When people would tell others about how upset they were with someone else, they would pit the person they told against the person they were complaining about. Somehow it validated them to know another person agreed they should be angry at person X over there who did _____ to them.

The aftermath was two people upset at person X and one party against another party.

I watched people leave church communities because others voiced their displeasure with people to third parties. It destroys. It doesn't bring freedom. It doesn't help us find what we're looking for.

ENVY

When you grapple with envy, you want what others have. You think if you lived on the side of the fence they live on, all would be freed up in your life.

But if you think the other side of the lawn is greener, you probably aren't spending time watering your own lawn.

Eventually what we own—or could own—starts to define us. Somehow it scratches an itch of freedom.

You have to be honest.

Don't you feel good when you buy a new gadget or trinket? Doesn't that new shirt or pair of pants make you feel good? It does—for about thirty minutes.

Isn't it weird how the newest iPhone or a brand-new car can make you feel good about yourself and your life?

But it never lasts.

Why is that?

Maybe by conquering stuff, we conquer an insecurity that tells us we are worth nothing. Owning stuff makes us feel worth more.

It goes beyond stuff too.

Envy makes us want our neighbor's spouse. The song "Jesse's Girl" wasn't just a catchy tune. We start looking at the other men and women, thinking that if we had them on our arm, we would somehow be complete. This is not a Tom Cruise movie. People don't complete us. We feed ourselves this lie that people *do* complete us, though, and that if we just had the right person, then we would be free.

We're imperfect beings, every single one of us, and as much as you have your insecurities, someone else has theirs. They're working through their issues, and they're going to mix their issues with yours.

How can they make *you* complete when they aren't complete themselves? Only God, who is perfect, can complete you.

DRUNKENNESS

Have you heard the saying, "They're hiding in a wine bottle"?

A lot of people medicate their lack of freedom by trying to find that freedom in getting drunk. We all know from watching the drunks around us that it doesn't bring freedom, but it does bring lots of misery.

I would venture to say that Paul is suggesting this goes beyond the idea of drinking too much alcohol. I think he is trying to lead us to see we can overdo something to find freedom, and it just doesn't work.

Isn't it interesting that Paul moves from the ladder rung of envy—thinking that what others have will make us free, that our stuff will complete us—to the idea of overusing what God has given us?

Overuse is a gluttonous existence that puts an over-abundance of expectation on something external to give us freedom. All it does is destroy at a higher rate.

Does it look like freedom when we're caught up in gluttonous excess?

ORGIES

Paul completes the ladder he started for us, moving from overdoing your stuff to overdoing your drinking—really, overdoing anything other than God—and now overdoing your sexual appetite. No one ever jumps right into an orgy. Sexual immorality always comes first. When we are so completely off track we begin to binge in areas we once dabbled in to bring us peace. We trick ourselves into thinking that if a small dose didn't work, maybe a big dose will. It leads us to the same destination. Bondage. Chains. Despair.

THERE'S A BETTER WAY

Here's how Paul finishes up his laundry list: "And things like these. I warn you, as I warned you before, that those who do such things will not inherit the kingdom of God" (Gal. 5:21).

Again, this was not meant to be an exhaustive list, but Paul is saying that when you think you can bring freedom into your life through the things you want to do or things of this earth, you will never live the life God has for you. Your insecurity will sabotage the life you're meant to have with God.

We tell ourselves the lie that these things will bring us freedom.

That is tough to read, because how do you know what freedom truly tastes like if you have never tasted it before?

How can you not read the list above and not go, "I'm out"?

I read it and see myself there. I see my defense mechanisms, my unhealthy ways of living, and my unhealthy reaches for freedom.

Am I destined to live a life other than the one God wants for me?

Is there no hope?

Does insecurity win?

No.

God has a plan for us.

God has redemption for us.

God has freedom to give to us.

God has something that we can never give ourselves.

The war rages inside us, but there is hope.

PART III

SIGNATURE

Chapter 6

LIFE WITH THE LIFE-GIVER

Not often, but every once in a while,
God brings us to a major turning
point—a great crossroads in our life.
From that point we either go toward
a more and more slow, lazy, and use-
less Christian life, or we become more
and more on fire, giving our utmost for
His highest—our best for His glory.[1]

—OSWALD CHAMBERS

117

J ACOB LEFT HOME at a time in life when the next step was to get married, have kids, and start providing.

It wasn't normal to leave your homeland to do this.

Jacob had to leave, though, to find a wife and establish his life separate from his father and mother, due to his brother wanting to kill him. During the time he was away from home, both of his parents passed away, and Jacob wasn't there to mourn their deaths. He wanted to save his own life, but he really lost everything he knew as life.

Some historians believe Jacob was gone for twenty-plus years before he started to head back to his homeland. He went back with all his wealth in tow: goats, donkeys, camels, sheep, lambs, horses, servants, children, and wives. An agreement was made with his father-in-law, a memorial was built to solidify the agreement, and both sides parted from each other.

Here's where we left off with Jacob.

In the desert.

Hauling everything he owns.

A very wealthy man.

A large family in tow.

On his way back to his homeland.

And something happens in his struggle with insecurity and humanity here. Something the writer of Genesis doesn't fully explain to us. Something mysterious. Something we can only guess at.

In the desert, on this cross-country journey, Jacob is met by angels of God (Gen. 32:1).

Now, the text doesn't say if it's in a dream, as it had been the first time he journeyed through the desert. The text doesn't say if it's a few messengers of God—angels—who strolled up to him, just like the ones who had visited his grandparents, Abraham and Sarah. The text doesn't say if it's a heat-induced vision.

All we know is that somehow, someway, angels of God again come to Jacob in the desert.

This is significant.

It's almost like bookends for us as readers of Jacob's story.

Jacob was confronted with God and angels on his way out of his homeland, and he has another angelic connection with God on his way back into his homeland.

And this time he does a few things similarly:

> Jacob went on his way, and the angels of God
> met him. And when Jacob saw them he said,
> "This is God's camp!" So he called the name of
> the that place Mahanaim.
> —GENESIS 32:1–2

Jacob names the place he meets the angels, just as he did before, and most scholars believe Jacob even built a memorial, just as he did before.

Another memorial.

But despite the similarities between the two

memorial-building scenarios, there is one big difference this time around.

This time Jacob doesn't demand anything from God.

He makes no vow.

He inserts no "if-then" clauses.

He makes no selfish attempt to secure things.

Absent from this story are Jacob's insecurities.

What happened?

Does he feel, because he has stuff now, that God has given him things so he must be secure?

Does he feel so important that God should meet with him?

What brought him to this place, inside himself, where we no longer see his insecurities sabotaging his life, as they always had before?

Where did the change come from?

I like the word *struggle* when we talk about our insecurities, because by the very definition and understanding of the word, two sides wrestle against each other. Sometimes one side prevails, and at other times the other side prevails, each for a time.

Jacob is in a struggle.

You are in a struggle.

I am in a struggle.

We are all in a struggle.

And right now in Jacob's story his insecurities are losing the struggle and freedom is winning.

I think I am 51 percent right in this or else I would get another opinion, but I believe, even though the text doesn't exactly specify this, that Jacob finally realized he had insecurities and that they were sabotaging his life.

What he does next is so telling:

> And Jacob sent messengers before him to Esau his brother in the land of Seir, the country of Edom, instructing them, "Thus you shall say to my lord Esau: Thus says your servant Jacob, 'I have sojourned with Laban and stayed until now. I have oxen, donkeys, flocks, male servants, and female servants. I have sent to tell my lord, in order that I may find favor in your sight.'"
>
> —GENESIS 32:3–5

Now most people will say Jacob was afraid his brother, Esau, wanted to kill him so he acted this way. However, this is the first time that we hear of Jacob wanting to interact with his brother since he left home so long ago. Jacob is journeying into uncertainty. He has no clue if Esau is even alive, let alone in good health. He has no idea if Esau's desire is to kill him.

All we know, as the readers of this story, is that Jacob's first words to his brother, via a messenger, are laced with humility and a desire to reconcile their relationship.

Notice in the statement sent to Esau that Jacob says these things:

"My lord Esau."

"Your servant Jacob."

"My lord."

"That I may find favor in your sight."

There is humility in his words.

There's honesty for a change.

Jacob even tells Esau what he's obtained while he's been gone, almost as if saying, "I'm not coming back home to try to take anything I stole from you via your birthright or the blessing I received from Dad. I have stuff. I'm not after stuff. All I want is to connect with you."

Can you see his statement to his brother now through this lens?

It's very unlike Jacob, according to everything we've seen in Jacob's life. There's no manipulation, no con, no selfish ambition.

Just a desire to restore what his insecurities had sabotaged.

The story continues:

> And the messengers returned to Jacob, saying, "We came to your brother Esau, and he is coming to meet you, and there are four hundred men with him." Then Jacob was greatly afraid and distressed. He divided the people

who were with him, and the flocks and herds
and camels, into two camps, thinking, "If Esau
comes to the one camp and attacks it, then the
camp that is left will escape."

—GENESIS 32:6–8

The messengers return with news that Esau is on his
way with four hundred men to meet Jacob.

Four hundred men!

Who brings four hundred men to say hi?

If you stole something from someone—not just once
but twice—and they headed your way with four hundred men, regardless of your intentions to reconcile
the relationship with them, you would be scared.

I would be too.

As I said earlier, what Jacob does is telling.

He prays.

And Jacob said, "O God of my father Abraham
and God of my father Isaac, O LORD who said
to me, 'Return to your country and to your
kindred, that I may do you good,' I am not
worthy of the least of all the deeds of stead-
fast love and all the faithfulness that you have
shown to your servant, for with only my staff
I crossed this Jordan, and now I have become
two camps. Please deliver me from the hand
of my brother, from the hand of Esau, for I
fear him, that he may come and attack me, the

mothers with the children. But you said, 'I will surely do you good, and make your offspring as the sand of the sea, which cannot be numbered for multitude.'"

—GENESIS 32:9–12

Jacob finds himself humbled before God and begging for God's protection. He remembers all God said to him in the past, and he isn't using any of the lame verbiage he used before about "if-then." Jacob wants God to protect him, and if God doesn't show up, it is going to be a train wreck in Jacob's mind.

The text goes on to tell us that Jacob sleeps on his request and plea to God, and in the morning he sends a gift to his brother, Esau. He sends the gift in segments, but here is the list of what he sends:

- Two hundred female goats
- Twenty male goats
- Two hundred ewes
- Twenty rams
- Thirty milking camels and their calves
- Forty cows
- Ten bulls
- Twenty female donkeys
- Ten male donkeys

Jacob starts to wipe his assets clean by giving all these things to his brother, Esau. Yes, he is trying to buy Esau's approval in a way, but it's rather amazing Jacob is willing to give his stuff away at all. When we first met Jacob, he was stealing things away from Esau. Now he's giving to Esau so much of what he has.

Something has clicked inside Jacob.

His stuff doesn't define him.

He doesn't need things to make him feel free from insecurity.

EVERYTHING IS MEANINGLESS

Remember Solomon?

That king of Israel had everything.

And I mean *everything*.

In Ecclesiastes, remember, Solomon writes what he's learned from having everything, being everything, and giving in to every fleshly desire. (I get excited about the book just writing that last sentence!)

He starts off the book like this:

> The words of the Preacher, the son of David, king in Jerusalem. Vanity of vanities, says the Preacher, vanity of vanities! All is vanity.
> —ECCLESIASTES 1:1–2

If only you and I understood Hebrew. The original language version of this passage means way more than what our English version of it communicates. The word *vanity* we see here is the Hebrew word *hebel*, which refers to something fleeting, such as a vapor or a mist, that doesn't last, is temporary, and is there for only a second.

If you think about it, that means it is pretty meaningless.

Solomon starts off by ranting: "Everything's meaningless and there for just a second—like a vapor that is gone so fast. Everything's meaningless!"

Everything?

Everything.

This guy had it all, did it all, saw it all, experienced it all—and he says it's all meaningless and temporary.

He goes on:

> What does man gain by all the toil at which he
> toils under the sun?
>
> —ECCLESIASTES 1:3

After saying that everything is fleeting and meaningless, Solomon asks this rhetorical question: What does all your hard work, all you're doing, all you're striving for, all your desires, all your time actually gain you on earth?

Well…he already gave us the answer.

It gains us nothing of meaning.

> All things are full of weariness; a man cannot
> utter it; the eye is not satisfied with seeing, nor

the ear filled with hearing. What has been is what will be, and what has been done is what will be done, and there is nothing new under the sun. Is there a thing of which it is said, "See, this is new"? It has been already in the ages before us.

—ECCLESIASTES 1:8–10

Solomon laments to the world that everything we encounter doesn't fulfill and doesn't bring freedom and that there's nothing new that will cure any of that.

It's all fleeting.

It's all meaningless.

The whole book he writes is about showing and proving this point.

In Ecclesiastes Solomon talks about how he had it all and it was just like having nothing. He was the same person. It didn't change anything. It didn't cure anything. It didn't make him better.

Do you get that?

Do you understand it?

If you could change all the external things about your life you want to change and fulfill all the internal desires you have, it wouldn't change the fact that you're still not free. Those efforts don't bring real freedom. They won't fix what you think they'll fix.

Sure, you can get the plastic surgery you think will cure the insecurity you have about your body. But it won't change the way you view yourself. It won't stop you from constantly worrying what others think about your body.

Sure, you can lie about who you are and make yourself into something you're not. But that won't change the way you feel about yourself. You'll still feel worthless and unsuccessful. You'll see others smile over your false accolades, but those smiles won't quench the desire for true worth that lives inside of you.

Sure, you can give yourself sexually to every person who wants your body. But doing so will never change the desire inside you for real love.

Sure, you can work your guts off to gain massive amounts of wealth. But getting wealth will never bring your soul freedom.

Sure, you can shy away from people. But in your isolation you'll never find the connections God intended for your life.

The job isn't going to give it to you.

The right partner isn't going to give it to you.

Neither will the right house.

The right clothes.

The highest achievements.

The best-looking body.

The most put-together look.

The flawless makeup.

It's all meaningless.

IT WON'T FREE YOU

I told you how I grew up.

Divorced parents.

Never feeling I was a part of either family.

These dynamics drove me to be a success—better than others at whatever I put my hand to do—because I wanted and needed the attention and acceptance in life. I figured if I got that, maybe I would be free from loneliness and rejection.

And did I ever work my guts out to prove I was good enough for someone to love and want!

I would like to think that I'm smart, but I have come to realize I'm of average intelligence—I just work harder than others. And school was where I first got the opportunity to try. I worked hard at every grade in elementary school, and when I realized in junior and senior high that we were graded in relation to each other, on a curve, I worked as hard as I could to get top scores in all my classes. I loved being the top grade on a test. I loved showing my parents how amazing my grades were versus the other students in school.

But it didn't free me.

I worked hard at playing sports, thinking maybe if I were a success there, it would give me the acceptance and attention I desired.

It didn't free me.

I worked hard in college, graduating *la-di-da*, or whatever it's called.

It didn't free me.

I worked hard at all my jobs, wanting to be the best employee.

It didn't free me.

I stepped into full-time vocational ministry, working seventy-hours-plus a week. I picked up on the standard of all the other pastors, and then did more. I read a book a week, perfected my public speaking, organized everything better than expected, never let anything get in the way of my goals, and did more than most could do in twenty years of ministry in a matter of eight years. (Someone said that to me when I finished up—please don't take it as pride on my part.)

It didn't free me.

I planted churches. I spoke all over the world. I spoke in big, big churches, and I spoke in small, small churches. I stayed in five-star hotels, and I stayed in barns. I ate at the finest restaurants, and I ate at gas stations. I got paid big money to speak, and I got no money to speak, paying for travel expenses out of my own pocket.

It didn't free me.

I lived in an eight-hundred-square-foot apartment, and I lived in a four-thousand-square-foot house. I had the big-screen TV with every possible channel, and I had a broken TV with no cable. I had it all at the end of my time as a church planter in Utah, and I had nothing when I left for college.

It didn't free me.

The lie we tell ourselves if we have too little is that if we get more, it will free us. The lie we tell ourselves if we have too much is that if we could just have less, it will free us. These two groups always look at each other and think the other is better off.

The poor look at the wealthy and think, "If I had what they had..."

The wealthy look at the poor and think, "If I had what they had..."

Solomon says he had it all and found it all meaningless.

I've had both and also found it all meaningless.

These goals and efforts don't bring you freedom.

They don't cure your insecurities.

SOMETHING'S BROKEN

Maybe, just maybe, this is what finally hit Jacob.

Had he acquired it all—riches, women, children, and power—and still felt the same inside? Was he walking through the desert, heading home, remembering how he left home with nothing but the clothes on his back, only to realize he still felt the same way now? Are scholars right in suggesting that the memorial he builds now as he's heading home is a bookend to the one he built on his way out?

I believe Jacob realizes he's been given all he asked God for and doesn't feel one bit different inside than he did when he asked for it. I believe this is the moment Jacob came to realize that all he has is meaningless in the grand scheme of life—that it will not free him from what he's been feeling since the day he was born.

It was all vain.

A vanity of vanities.

Track with me here, because I want to open this up for us to see, and to do that we have to go back to the very beginning of human existence—because this struggle, this back and forth, is almost interlaced into our very being.

In Genesis, when God makes man and woman, He sets them in the Garden of Eden and instructs them not to eat of one tree in the whole garden.

Just one.

Satan comes along, disguised as a snake, and tells Eve, the first woman, that if they eat from this one tree, their "eyes will be opened, and [they] will be like God, knowing good and evil" (Gen. 3:5).

Most of us know the story, even if we haven't spent any time in church. The woman eats from the tree, and the man does too. Sin, disobedience, and separation from God enter the world.

And they enter because man and woman, Adam and Eve, at the very beginning of human existence, thought that if they ate of this one tree, they could be godlike, could know what God knows, and could know what was right and wrong for life.

In other words, sin entered the world because Adam and Eve wanted to control things and not let God control them.

God finds Adam and Eve hiding with shame in the garden after their fruit fest. He rebukes them, which is a fancy church word for scorning them for their actions, and then He tells them that with their disobedience comes consequences—curses for their actions.

God tells Eve, who is representative of all women, that she will be cursed with pain in childbirth. With pain in being a mom. And with longing for her husband to make her feel complete.

Every woman knows childbirth is a painful process, and any mother knows that raising children is painful. Your love for them makes it so you hurt when they hurt and rejoice when they rejoice. In some sense, mothers gain security from their children.

And if you live on any other planet, you will not know this, but all of us on earth know that women find a sense of completeness, security, and worth in a man. A man makes or breaks a woman—and not just when it comes to marriage. It starts with childhood, in a daughter's relationship with her father.

Now, I'm going to generalize here, and I know generalizations are muddy water.

But I couldn't help but notice two very glaring realities of fathers giving their daughters worth when I traveled across the United States. For one, I spent a lot of time at a drop-in shelter for homeless youth in Denver, Colorado, called Sox Place. I served on the board for a while, and I loved this place. They feed the homeless youth of Denver a meal every day and give them a place to get out of the extreme weather conditions in the summers and winters. They also supply the youth with clothing and hygiene needs and get them on their feet with finding jobs or schooling.

Over the years I talked with a lot of the homeless kids at Sox Place, and what I observed with the females caught my attention. None of them—now, I know there are exceptions—had a connection with their fathers while they were growing up.

None.

Similarly, while working on a pilot television show for a local television station in Utah, we were assigned to interview the guys who were working at XXXchurch .com. They were going to the largest porn convention in the world in Las Vegas, and we were going to meet up with them there to do the interview. While there, we also were going to interview some of the most well-known porn stars in the business.

As we were doing the interviews with the girls, I started having flashbacks to my talks with the homeless girls at Sox Place—reason being, none of the women in the porn business we interviewed had relationships with their fathers either. In fact, as I noticed this trend in the conversations, I asked our main reporter to specifically ask them to talk about their relationships with their fathers.

It didn't exist.

The curse for women, then, seems to make their children and the men in their lives—fathers and husbands—the major source of their security and self-worth.

When it comes to men, God told Adam, the representative for men: "You will have to work for your survival. You will be cursed with work."

It doesn't take a rocket scientist to know that men throw themselves into their work. They find fulfillment in what they accomplish and what they do as it relates to their jobs.

Just listen to a man when he meets another man socially. The first question he asks the other is usually, "What do you do?" And we all know this has to do with work.

A nonworking man shrivels up as a person and is miserable. His sense of self-worth and identity was so tied to his job that the curse eats him up. Feeling worthless starts to eat at him from the inside out.

God said man was not complete by himself, that it was not good for man to be alone, and so from the very beginning He formed woman to be that other half. Not only does a man find his fulfillment in his work, then, for which he toils and labors only to receive pain in return, but he also finds his fulfillment in being with his other half—woman.

The problem here, though, is that God is usually left out of that equation.

See, in Genesis, when things were perfect and the way God intended them to be, man and woman were together, created by God to be helpers and companions to each other and to be complete together. In our fallen world, though, when God is taken out of that equation, men try to find their fulfillment by connecting with other women. This is why so many men can jump from woman to woman, conquering their other half, looking for a sense of fulfillment. Men live off the longing women have for them, but they don't know how to translate it back into security without God.

Without God in the picture it never leads to true security and freedom.

Women need men, and men need women. Their security is grafted together, but the fallen world sabotages the way that shared dependence was meant to be.

To say something is broken with humanity is an understatement. We all know something is broken. Our insecurities prove it to us.

Life, Corrected

Jesus said, "I came that they may have life and have it abundantly" (John 10:10).

These lives we're living? They're a mere existence.

To really be free—to have the life we long for inside of us—is to find it with Jesus.

He sets us free.

He corrects what went wrong in the garden.

He gets us out of mere existence and into real *life*.

The world—and maybe even the church—has taken the words and teachings of Jesus and turned Him into a flesh management coach. That's not what He is. He changes us. We don't change ourselves.

We need to get out of the Garden of Eden mentality. We aren't God, and we can't change creation.

But God—through Jesus Christ—can.

Because this curse, this humanity, this insecurity is woven inside of us, no amount of flesh management and rules and hoops and regulations will ever fix it. The only way for it ever to be fixed is for a life-giver to change it. And that is exactly what Jesus is offering and says He will do.

Jesus is a life-giver.

So this life-giving Savior changes us; we don't change ourselves.

And because things change inside us, things change outside us too.

Our realization of our insecurity is a realization that something is broken and wrong with the world. Our realization that we have to stop making this all about us is a realization that we aren't God and we need to let God rule and reign. Our realization that we have to stop comparing ourselves to others is a realization that everything is a fleeting vapor of meaninglessness existence.

Meaning and depth and freedom and security all come from Jesus, and Jesus alone!

While you and I were still—and some of us still are—walking around in our envy, our fear, our insecurity, our troubles, our hurt, our brokenness, our drunkenness, our rivalries, our hatred, our sexual immorality, our fits of rage, and our desire-soaked existence, Christ died for us.

He died to reconcile us to freedom.

He died to change our insides.

He died to save us from ourselves.

And when you locate the Savior and bow yourself to His rule and reign, He begins to remove the futility and vanity and insecurity from your soul. He begins to let you taste what real freedom is all about and what real life is all about. He begins to show you life separated from stuff, hurt, people's opinions, caste systems, and fleeting attempts for freedom.

I wish I could tell you the steps to take once Jesus intersects with your life, but that is the point of all of this—you can't do anything.

It is Jesus doing a miracle-working power in your life.

It's Time to Start Over

I thought I knew Jesus.

I knew a lot *about* Jesus.

I could tell you all about Him, much like I could tell you all about John Elway, my childhood sports hero. Where he went to high school and college. What year he got drafted and by whom. That he had been on his way to play professional baseball because he wasn't happy with the team that drafted him. The trade that kept him in the NFL playing football instead of playing baseball. On and on I can go about what I know about John Elway.

I know a lot *about* John Elway, but I don't *know* John Elway.

In the same way I knew a lot *about* Jesus, but I didn't *know* Jesus.

Until one day.

One day I stopped trying to cure all the hurts inside me and started to let Him inside me.

I knew there was something wrong inside.

I knew I couldn't do it and that the life I was living wasn't meant to be about me.

I knew that everything around me was meaningless without God.

And in those moments—in those moments with Jesus piercing my heart—things began to feel free. It was as if I finally got to taste the real butter.

I had no idea life was like this.

If anyone tries to tell you it happens in a single moment and then all is well, they are a liar. This life with Jesus is something you live out every day.

You have to focus your eyes on Him every day.

You have to let Him into your heart every day.

You have to let Him do spiritual surgery on you every day.

And after many, many days of this life-giver invading your life, it starts to get easier. It starts to be second nature. And this faith thing start to make sense.

Maybe that lawyer who approached Jesus was onto something by quoting from Deuteronomy: "'You shall love the Lord your God with all your heart and with all your soul and with all your strength and with all your mind, and your neighbor as yourself'" (Luke 10:27).

Think about heart, soul, strength, and mind in these terms: feelings, being, effort, and thoughts.

Maybe the key to letting Jesus give us the life He intended for us—freedom from insecurity, hurt, pain, rejection, and the like—is to focus our feelings, our being, our efforts, and our thoughts on God.

It seems as if this is what Jesus was always teaching people about—how to do this in light of their humanity. Why not look at those He hung out with the most, the ones who got to hear and see His practical applications for life? Looking at them can teach us so much about us and how to receive the life Jesus really offers. I've always tried to look at what the earlier followers did as my healthy example for life.

In the same way, surround yourself with those who speak and teach about Jesus today.

Learn, read, and listen to everything Jesus said.

Pray—day and night—to God.

Care about what God cares about.

Rejoice in what God rejoices for.

Mourn for what God mourns for.

Maybe, just maybe, in that moment in the desert, Jacob realized everything he ever thought would give him freedom was meaningless. And maybe it was in that moment of praying for God to save him from Esau that he knew only God could ever give him the true security and true freedom he'd been searching for.

I'm pretty sure that's what happened.

Chapter 7

THE LIFE YOU ALWAYS WANTED

Trust is the fruit of a relationship in
which you know you are loved.[1]
—William Paul Young

M Y YOUNGEST DAUGHTER, Berlyn, gets scared easier than her older sister. She will not go upstairs by herself or run into a crowd of people she doesn't know. She is the most timid of any of us in the family.

What's remarkable, in light of this, is the way she becomes the boldest, most secure person in the world when she's with me, holding my hand, curled up in my lap, or just next to my side. Hands down, the boldest.

Her boldness can be seen in the normal movements of life, like the time she was in tears, afraid to walk into a room that was dark by herself, but after I gave her a pep talk and stood in the hallway, she marched into that room and turned the light on as if she owned the place.

Her boldness can be seen in the funny moments in life as well. Like when we were in Costa Rica, heading down to the pool at our hotel, hand in hand, and as we were walking to the pool, a lady in a bikini came walking up the stairs toward us. Berlyn took one look at her and turned toward me. She squeezed my hand and said to me as loud as she could, "Dad, that lady has really big _____." It was if she knew she shouldn't say something about anyone out loud, but since I was with her, she could do whatever she wanted to do.

She has an amazing connection with me, her father.

All it takes is my presence.

A gentle hug.

An encouraging word.

An instruction to go and do.

In my presence all the timidity and insecurity are erased.

Why?

Because she trusts me.

There is trust between us.

She will dive off the side of any pool into my arms. If the world is scaring her, all she has to do is crawl into my arms and she is completely fulfilled and safe. If I send her to bed at night, it might take thirty minutes for her to fall asleep, but if I let her lie in my arms to go to sleep, it takes only minutes.

All because of trust.

If you have spent anytime in church you have heard the word *faith* thrown around. It's an esoteric word, to some degree. I think we all want to say we completely understand what it means, but if I asked you to define it and to tell me how you do it in your life, you would most likely stumble and ramble through the conversation.

To tell me that reading the Bible is faith is wrong.

To tell me that praying is faith is wrong.

To tell me that going to church is faith is wrong.

To tell me religion is faith is wrong.

Faith is a belief, but it is beyond knowledge.

Faith is an action, but it is beyond a checklist.

Faith is trust.

Trust in something you can't prove by measurable standards.

Trust in something you can't see.

Faith is trust.

The writer of Hebrews in the New Testament said this: "Now faith is the assurance of things hoped for, the conviction of things not seen" (Heb. 11:1).

The Message version of the Bible translates that same verse like this: "The fundamental fact of existence is that this trust in God, this faith, is the firm foundation under everything that makes life worth living."

And here is the crazy part of all this faith and trust talk.

Neither one exists without action.

I can say I trust something, but if I don't act on that belief, I really don't trust it. I just have rhetoric—meaningless rhetoric. That's like saying I love my wife and then doing everything opposite of what you would do if you loved someone. I wouldn't really love her in that case. I would just have meaningless rhetoric.

This faith—this word we use and hear all the time in our Jesus communities—has big implications for overcoming the sabotage of insecurity in our lives.

Paul said this to the Galatians when he was explaining faith to them and how important faith is to establishing the life God intends for us:

> Know then that it is those of faith who are the
> sons of Abraham. And the Scriptures, fore-
> seeing that God would justify the Gentiles
> by faith, preached the gospel beforehand to
> Abraham, saying, "In you shall all the nations
> be blessed." So then, those who are of faith are
> blessed along with Abraham, the man of faith.
> —GALATIANS 3:7–9

Paul is speaking out against two groups of people
here. The first is those who think they can gain freedom
on their own. The second is those who think they can
gain freedom because of who they are—because they
have the right lineage or pedigree, so to speak.

Paul says no to both of these things.

He does point to Jacob's grandfather, Abraham, as
an example, though. Paul says, "Abraham trusted God
and the nations are blessed because of it and those
who trust like Abraham will be blessed too!"

I read something like this, and I immediately want
to grab Paul by his head, look him in the eyes, and
demand to know what the blessing will be if I trust as
Abraham trusted.

What was Abraham's blessing?

Do we all get the same thing?

Is it freedom?

What appears to me when I read all of Paul's writings in light of Jesus's teachings is that Paul is trying to
convince his readers of this: If you trust God, then you

will have that abundant life Jesus taught about. You will experience the kingdom of heaven right here and now on earth.

When you hear that God can give you freedom, do you trust Him to do so?

When you hear that God can cure your insecurities, do you trust Him to do so?

For some of us there are moments that we throw in the towel of trying to live this life on our own, realizing it is beyond our control, and trust God. Maybe that was what Jacob did as he sat in the desert on his way back to his homeland.

When you experience one of those moments, you remember it forever. It is a calendar moment—something that sticks with you forever.

One of my dearest friends, Brendan Perko (whom I just call Perko), had one of those moments in his life. He can tell you the date and time when he woke up early in the morning just knowing God was speaking to his soul. He can tell you exactly what he felt God pressing into him.

He says God woke him up and said, "What are you doing with your life?"

Perko called me that day to tell me what God said to him, and since then I've had the privilege of watching him walk in a trusting relationship with God. Are there ups and downs in his life? Yes. He's human. But he keeps his eyes focused on trusting God.

It's been like night and day as you examine Perko's life now versus what it was in the past.

Some of us have throw-in-the-towel moments too—those moments we can point to that are red-letter-days on our calendars of remembrance.

For others of us there are no distinct moments. There is just a passage of time. We slowly start to trust God in areas of our lives and slowly start to follow God. There is no night-and-day story to our lives—just a long, complicated story of walking with God over a continuous period. We gather bumps and bruises and lessons learned, and we slowly, over time, take our hands off the wheel of life and trust God.

The "exact moment" people? They are the exception to the rule. And they too will live out a process of being transformed from the inside out into what God intends their lives to look like.

It's like cooking a cake in an oven. At what point, exactly, is it a cake? When it's being mixed? When it's starting to rise?

Maybe the "exact moment" people are those who get all the ingredients in the bowl at the same time, which means the cake enters the oven sooner. Maybe the rest of us are those who slowly add the ingredients into the bowl. It just takes a little longer for everything to be ready to place in the oven.

Sanctification—that fancy church word for your transformation as you walk with God—just takes time.

And before you know it, you find transformation in your life. Things are further along then you ever thought they would be. Things have changed. Some areas are complete. Some are still in development. Some areas of insecurity are gone. Others are still sensitive.

START WITH FOCUS

That was me.

All the ingredients were put together in my life to follow God, but the process took time, just as it takes time for a cake to finish baking. I'm not even sure when mine was complete. It's almost as if I woke up one day, looked back, and went, "Wow. I'm trusting God and seeing the blessing—the abundant life—actually come out of me!"

That's doesn't mean there aren't struggles. I am human, after all.

Sanctification has been about a passage of time that slowly changed things in my life. I didn't start full on trusting God one day, with immediate physical evidence pouring out of my soul and heart.

The process was slow. But it did happen.

And I can tell you this. The process of sanctification—the transformation from my insecurities—started happening when I focused. When I realized I was striving for freedom in my life and only God could give me freedom. When I realized I even needed freedom.

When I realized my insecurities were destroying the relationships around me.

My relationship with God wasn't what it was supposed to be.

My relationships with others weren't what they were supposed to be.

I didn't even like myself.

But as I focused and turned one area of life after another over to God in complete trust, things started to change.

Mine wasn't a reckless abandonment kind of trust some have the ability for. I had to start slow, methodically handing over this area, then that area, then another area over to God, which eventually led to the whole of my life being blessed.

For instance, remember the story I told you in chapter 1 about my parents being divorced and me not feeling like I was ever a part of their families? I had a very destructive relationship with my stepdad for the longest time because of that. But when I started to focus on my trust and transformation in God, I decided I would trust God to heal that area of my life.

I stopped looking at my past and started focusing on where God was taking me. And as I kept practicing and living out what I was reading from Jesus in the area of relationships, the pain I always felt in my heart from my stepdad and the anger that was always swelling in me toward him was...gone.

I have no clue how it left.

I have no clue where it went.

I do know God took it away.

I'm not sure when it happened, but one day I noticed it was gone.

Now, I used to hate my stepdad. I wished for his death and despised everything about him. But now I hurt when he hurts and rejoice when he rejoices. I love him and wish for his well-being in all he does. He has placed me as the executor of his estate, and I have become one of his confidants in life.

A relationship restored, mended, and healed, all because of trust in God.

Is my whole life one big area of trust?

Not every day, and not in every area all the time.

Maybe this is what it means to be human and to live in a fallen world.

I still struggle.

I still learn.

I still have to empty myself.

I still have to put myself to death.

I still have to push *reset*.

It is in these times of going back, of emptying ourselves, of realizing who we are and who God is, of thrusting our trust at God that He gives us a life full of freedom.

Clear It Down to Nothing

I think it makes sense to say that if you allow additives in your trust in God, then you border on not really trusting God. Thus, your life with God will not bring you the intended results you are striving for.

Trust in God most be void of additives.

There must be nothing before there can be something.

God likes to work in the nothingness.

Remember how Genesis starts off? By telling us the world was void and without form—and then creates. God took the nothingness of the ground and made humanity. Out of the nothingness—the emptiness— God works, creates, and makes things happen.

That seems to be exactly what happened to Jacob as he sat in the desert too.

He emptied himself of his possessions to his brother.

He emptied out his desires to God.

He was left with nothing.

If you've ever planted a fruit tree—or any tree, for that matter—you know you have to make sure there's nothing else growing in the spot you plant the seed. If there is, it will suck up all the water and nutrients in the soil, leaving none for the seed. You have to clear out the area where you want your new fruit tree to grow.

As the tree sprouts forth from the ground, weeds eventually come up in that area too, and if you're not careful, you'll run into the same problems you had in the beginning—lack of nutrients and water. You have to pull up those weeds and get them away from your young fruit tree if you don't want them to choke out the new tree.

A fruit tree starts with nothing.

And after time, it produces fruit.

Some fruit trees and bushes produce fruit very fast. Others take long to produce their fruit. All trees and bushes are different.

I planted some raspberry bushes in my backyard one year, and it took until the next year to see any fruit. Or consider the asparagus. Though it's a superfood, it must be the loneliest of all vegetables—no one likes it. Asparagus takes two years to yield a harvest.

This is what it's like to trust God.

Just as Paul listed out the ways we try to find freedom on our own, which we already covered, he also lists out the fruit that forms in our lives if we trust God. He starts off his list by saying this: "But the fruit of the Spirit is..." (Gal. 5:22). In other words, he's saying, "Here is what God will bless your life with..." And then, just as he gave us a ladder of fleshly desires we think will bring us freedom, he gives us a string of fruit that will start to be produced in our lives.

Now, as you read this list and see what Paul is talking about, notice what these things are. You'll notice they're all the areas we have wanted that freedom to come—all those things we're so insecure about and want freedom from.

Paul is going to show you that God will give you those things if you learn to trust Him.

LOVE

In our culture we use the word *love* for everything under the sun.

"I love Doritos."

"I love my college football team."

"I love the beach."

"I love my spouse."

How is it possible we are saying the same thing here? We love our spouse, and we love Doritos?

This word has become so interchangeable in our culture. We interchange it for words such as *like, admire,* or *enjoy.*

Even when we are using the word *love* in the correct way, such as to talk about our spouses, it is usually used to mean, "Because this person gives back to me or does this for me or has these qualities, I love them." All you have to do to see that our use of the word *love* has some pretty self-seeking qualities is to be in a relationship that gets to the point of one of you asking the other, "Tell me why you love me."

"I love you because you are pretty."

So if she wasn't pretty enough for you, you wouldn't love her?

"I love you because you're romantic."

So if he didn't know how to romance you, you wouldn't love him?

"I love you because you're a great cook."

So if they couldn't cook, it would be over?

When we do use the word *love*, it's usually in response to external conditions.

That's not what Paul is talking about when he uses the word *love* in his list of the fruits of the Spirit. He's actually using the Greek word *agape*, which has been translated into *love* because it's the only word in our English language close to its meaning. Yet the meaning of *agape* goes far beyond the way we use the word *love* in our culture or language.

Agape would best be understood in light of our examples above if you were using it to say, "I don't love you because you're pretty or romantic or a great cook. I love you because... well, for no reason other than that inside me, I want to honor you, serve you, give to you, walk with you, be with you, and make your life better."

This is the love Paul says God brings into your life when you trust Him.

It's a love that's not about external conditions or qualities.

It's a love that just exists.

The main school of thought during the time Paul wrote this passage was that it was dangerous to love. If you loved little things, it would cause you to love big things, and if you reversed that—didn't love little things—then you wouldn't love the big things of life, either, and you could lose them and be OK. One day your health or your kids or your job would be taken from you, and the absence of love would make it easier to cope with those days of big losses.

Aristotle taught that love is weakened when you give it to too many—thus, he said you should give love to only a few. If you distributed too much love to others, he said it cheapened the value of your love. It's like flooding the economy with your love so that the supply exceeded the demand.

Jesus taught the opposite of what everyone else was saying during the early first century—and has been saying ever since—when it comes to love. He said that real love is willing to risk it all and should be shared with everyone. Real love is not meant only for those in our "Fab Five," in other words.

It's a love that risks.

It's a love that includes.

It's a love that is a choice, rather than a feeling or emotion.

Trusting God—following after His Son, Jesus—produces this type of love in us.

And this same love is what we experience from God.

You are loved not because of anything you can do for God but because He created you.

You are His.

He chooses to love you.

He has included you in His love.

He loves you with the risk that you will never repay His love.

God loved Jacob even when Jacob was throwing bargains in God's face, saying, "I'll only love You as my God if You do this for me." God smiled back and still loved.

When we experience unloving moments from others in this world, the lie we tell ourselves is that we are unloved. But the reality is that we are loved by the only person who really matters: God.

God loves you.

He's happy with you.

You can do nothing to make Him happier with you.

He loves you right now, as you are—not a future version of yourself.

Trusting God—following His Son, Jesus—will help you realize this amazing truth.

You are *loved*.

There's a great movie titled *Invincible* that's based on the true story of Vince Papale, who responded to an open tryout to play for the Philadelphia Eagles. Vince, portrayed by Mark Wahlberg, ends up being the only person who is invited to the training camp. These scenes keep coming up where Vince looks at a note his wife left in their house after she cleaned it out and left him, filing for divorce. The note reads, "You'll never go anywhere, never make a name for yourself, and never make any money." The realization for the audience is that Vince is reading this note to inspire himself to push through all the pain and heartache he's experiencing as an outsider trying to make the roster of an NFL team.

Spoiler alert. At the end of the movie Vince makes the roster for the Eagles and is about to play in the first home game of the season. His teammates still haven't really accepted him, as he is not a professional but a guy off the street. He's about to leave the locker room and take the field for the start of the game, and he pulls the note from his locker again. He reads it and then crumples it up. His new girlfriend and his friends have been by his side the whole time, and he realizes in that moment that what his wife said was a form of motivation but not the motivation he actually needed to be himself.

When Vince takes the field for the game, there's something different about him. On the opening kickoff, he makes the big tackle and immediately points to his girlfriend and friends, who are sitting up in the stands. He knows he is loved, and he has people who believe in him. He plays like a pro and wins the game for the Eagles.

Trusting God is like crumpling up what the world has said to you and realizing the greatness of the love you have on your side.

You have Someone who believes in you.

You are *loved*.

JOY

Joy is the next thing on the vine of fruit Paul says will be produced in our lives when we trust God.

I think it's easy to think the word *joy* means "happiness," but it goes beyond the emotion of just feeling happy. Joy is that deep happiness and confidence that everything is OK, no matter the situation.

Joy is not prompted by favorable circumstances.

Joy is not prompted by unfavorable circumstances.

Joy is the knowledge, the faith, the confidence that everything is OK in the grand scheme of things because God is in control.

This is why Solomon could say that everything is meaningless but still want to walk with and serve God. He knew deep-seated happiness, regardless of extremely favorable circumstances or devastating events. Why? Because God picks the ingredients of life, and God is in control. A grander perspective was available but invisible to the naked eye of humanity; we naturally cannot see God's point of view—only our small perspective. It is like putting your thumb as close as you can to your face and trying to see what is behind it. You will see only your thumb and not the big picture. Solomon began to realize that if he could pull back the thumb, there was a bigger picture to see, but that process was not a natural habit of our humanity. Joy comes with seeing a bigger picture.

As you trust God and follow Jesus, you start to see this fruit of joy in your life. It will shock you when it appears, because what once would destroy your day is now just a bump in the pavement. Things of this world will not control your happiness, but knowing God does.

What amazing freedom God brings to our lives when this fruit starts to sprout!

Freedom from pain.

Freedom from others controlling our emotions.

Freedom from despair.

God has everything under control. He's not shocked by what comes up in our lives, and He has a bigger plan that we cannot see. He picks the ingredients of life and mixes together a great recipe that, when finished, will be a masterful main course.

Take joy in knowing that no matter what happens, God is working things out.

God has a bigger plan than you can see.

God is in control.

PEACE

The string of fruit continues in Paul's writing as he adds peace.

The Greek word Paul uses here, *eir'nē*, refers to an absence of alienation or a state of reconciliation. It's an inner contentment, much like joy but with deeper meaning.

The Jews used a Hebrew word for peace, *shalom*, and it has deep meaning. It is not just the absence of conflict but also a deep inner sense of well-being. Paul was most likely referring to this word and its meaning with his writings on the fruit of peace.

In the Old Testament we read the story of Job, who loses everything in a very unusual way. First, his donkeys, his oxen, and all his servants are destroyed by a tribe that attacks them. Just as Job is getting the news about this loss, another servant runs up and says that fire fell from the sky and burned up all of Job's sheep and the servants who were watching over them. It's a bad day when not only people attack your livestock but also fire falls from the sky and destroys more of your stuff.

But it doesn't end there. As one servant finishes vomiting up troubles, another servant runs up and delivers more bad news.

His kids were killed.

His grandchildren were killed.

His house was destroyed.

His wealth was wiped out.

Then, after all this has been taken from him, his health goes.

There's this scene where Job has just heard the news from all his servants that he has lost all his possessions and all his family. He tears his clothes, shaves his head, and throws himself to the ground in mourning. He cries out, "The LORD gave, and the LORD has taken away; blessed be the name of the LORD" (Job 1:21).

Eventually Job's wife tells him to curse God for all that has been taken from his life. Job's friends even get in on the action, telling Job to stop trusting God.

But Job refuses to turn his back on the trust he has for God.

Despite losing everything, there is *shalom* in Job's life because of his trust in God.

Think of the word *peace* as a sense of complete contentment in your surroundings, situation, and life.

Peace that you can have everything and you are OK.

Peace that you can lose everything and you are OK.

Peace that you are pretty enough.

Peace that you are good enough.

Peace that you are strong enough.

Peace that you are brave enough.

Peace that you are the second son.

In reality we can only speculate about Jacob's inner developments as he sat in the desert, but it appears he was starting to trust God and that God was beginning to cultivate peace in his life right away.

God brings the freedom of peace into your life.

We tell ourselves the lie that we will never have this freedom—that it is too lofty of a height to reach, that we will just learn to deal with being discontent with flesh management techniques, but the reality is that God will cultivate this peace—sometimes supernaturally—in your inner being if you walk with Him in trust.

PATIENCE

This Greek word Paul uses here, *makrothumía*, means "patience to put up with people."

We are all broken people with flaws and struggles. We ram into each other daily and cause destruction in each other's lives. But God produces the ability in our heart's eye to give a gentle understanding to the realities of our common humanity and give others time, as well as grace, to mature beyond their mistakes to us.

Foolish people are going to be foolish.

Haters gonna hate.

People are flawed.

But God helps you deal with them.

My friend Matt and his wife, Jamie, adopted a dog that was kept in very bad living situations. This dog developed an overwhelming fear for humans she doesn't know—the complete opposite of my dog, who was raised in a very loving, active, and social family. My dog wants to meet every new person in the world, but my friend Matt's dog doesn't want to get near you. If you get close to her, she turns and looks the other way, trying to let you know she is ignoring you.

It's easy from my perspective and the information

Matt has given me about her developmental process to understand her timidity with humans. I'm patient with her, not expecting her to act like my dog but seeing her actions as a result of the life she's lived. It will take lots of time spent with her and lots of grace from me for us to make progress in making a connection.

That is what it's like with every single one of us. If we could see the developmental processes all of us have gone through and the lives we have lived, we would understand why we do what we do to one another.

Paul says God gives us the ability to give time and grace—patience—to those around us, and possibly the ability to see the bigger picture of who they are and why they are the way they are. Our interactions with others becomes guided by this bigger picture of understanding, and we don't abandon them so quickly or run from trying to develop better relationships with them.

The lie we tell ourselves is that people will just hurt us—that it's unavoidable. The truth is that people are messy—all of us are—and that we all need time and grace in our lives.

KINDNESS

Kindness is a gentle and sweet disposition.

We all know what it feels like to interact with someone who is kind. If you used everything they did as an example of what kindness is, you wouldn't necessarily agree that the list added up to a definition of kindness, but that's because kindness is best understood by how a person makes you feel.

"They were kind to me," we find ourselves thinking.

Someone can pat your hand in an assuring way, but the person who passes on the *feeling* of gentleness to you is the one you would call kind. It might be the look they give you, the smile they share with you, the paused moment of understanding they pass with you.

Kindness is the loss of one's own interests in caring more about the feelings of others.

Kindness bites its tongue when it comes to voicing opinions or hurting the feelings of others.

Kindness pauses life to care about the small things others are engaged in.

Kindness makes the atmosphere pleasant for all.

Kindness flows.

It's infectious.

It spreads.

And Paul says that if you trust God, this fruit will be produced in your life. The kindness of God is passed to us, then from us to others, and then from others to even more.

GOODNESS

Kindness and goodness seem to be interchangeable, but they're actually different.

We said kindness is a feeling you give to others.

Goodness is about moral uprightness.

It's doing what's right, moving others to moral virtue, and keeping what is right, right.

Kindness is *how* you do it; goodness is *what* you do.

I've met a lot of people holding picket signs who have good moral points to their cause, but all their goodness is devoid of kindness.

You can keep your moral virtues intact and still be mean and cold.

You can be kind and caring but completely deviant in your morals.

Paul says you get both fruits when you trust God. God forms in you the ability to make others feel your kindness and, at the same time, stand for what is right and good.

FAITHFULNESS

Think about this word as *loyalty*.

Does it come as a shock to you that Paul, in talking about what happens when we have faith, or trust, in God, says the Spirit of God produces fruit that is a fullness of that trust—in other words, loyalty?

God gives you the ability to be completely loyal in your trust.

How amazing is that?

Sociologists call it habit, but maybe there's something more spiritual to the human condition of repetition. Maybe through our repetition, God has wired us to form loyalty. Maybe, through Paul, God is exposing this programming to the world.

It isn't just a loyalty *toward* God, either.

You start to feel the loyalty that has always existed toward you *from* God.

He has always been there for you.

He will always be there for you.

You cannot outrun Him.

You cannot do anything that keeps Him from being your God.

The whole world might abandon you. The whole world might shun you. The whole world might smile and stab you in the back.

But God never will.

Ever.

God is a loyal God.

And the fruit of your trust in Him is the growing understanding that He is always there for you, always wanting you on His team.

Remind yourself not only of God's love for you every day, but also of His loyalty toward you every day.

He's cheering you on.

He's in your corner.

He isn't leaving your side when you mess up.

He isn't leaving your side when the world says you aren't pretty enough.

He isn't leaving your side when you don't have enough money.

He isn't leaving your side when you don't talk the way everyone else talks.

He isn't leaving your side when your clothes don't fit the style of the culture.

It could be argued that this fruit might be one of the most refreshing of all the fruits to experience, next to love and peace.

You're not alone.

God is with you.

Always.

GENTLENESS

Gentleness does not mean weakness.

In fact, being gentle is not a lack of strength but the presence of strength under control.

If you were to pick up a baby rabbit, you might be told to be gentle with it. The thought is that you have the strength to hurt the baby rabbit, and you are being asked to put that strength under control and treat it with less strength than you have the ability to produce.

We've developed a colloquialism in our American culture with the phrase, "He's a big teddy bear." The meaning is completely understood in our culture as we envision a large, strong man who is gentle.

A man who controls his strength with others around him.

A man who looks as though he can use his strength at any time but has harnessed it for use only when needed.

How wild is it that God fosters in us the fruit of taking whatever strength we have and being able to control it?

SELF-CONTROL

Here we are at the last fruit of the Spirit Paul lists for us: self-control.

I've often wondered if he listed it last for a reason. The word in the Greek, *enkrateia*, means "to have mastery over the body's appetites, sex, food, mind, actions."

Could it be that Paul knows the desires and the defense mechanisms we usually run to, hoping they bring us freedom, become easier to control when we have been walking in a trusting relationship with God over a period of time, because God has given us the ability to control them? Could it be this fruit of self-control brings us the ultimate freedom from being stuck in a cycle of destruction?

Paul says self-control will be produced in your life when you trust God.

Your desires will not go away, but you will be able to master them.

Remember, it is in the nothing that God can produce something. It is in the nothing that God likes to work. To cultivate fruit, God needs you to trust Him to be the one to produce these freedom-giving fruits of life— the abundant life—in your world.

Maybe the nothing is the only thing that works because then you cannot give credit to any other source but God.

Maybe the nothing is the only thing that works because then God can really show off.

Maybe the nothing is the only thing that works because then you have no distractions.

Whatever the reason, whether by a single moment or a time period of life, if you empty yourself and trust God, He will bring you freedom from all those insecurities.

The sabotage only lasts until you enter into the nothing.

The sabotage only lasts until you start trusting God.

Chapter 8

WHAT IS YOUR NAME?

Always be a first-rate version of yourself, instead of a second-rate version of somebody else.[1]
—JUDY GARLAND

My true identity
has fled me,
fled me to another
to my friends and family
my true identity
is all that makes me.[2]

—CYRUS DIAZ

WHAT I DIDN'T tell you about my childhood is this. My insecurity grew so strong that I started disliking the very name I was given at birth. What boy is named Trinity? Even today I still get asked if I was named after *The Matrix* movies.

Not only did I not fit in with my family as a kid or with the kids in each state we moved to, I didn't fit in with anyone when it came to the very name I had. No one was named Trinity, and even when the name grew popular because of the Keanu Reeves movies, it was always girls who were named Trinity.

Why did I have to be named *Trinity?*

Why not some tough-sounding name like Maxwell? Then I could go by Max for short.

Why not something basic and simple—something that would blend me into my cultural environment— like the name Steve? It isn't a good rapper's name, but I didn't want to be a rapper.

Or here's a better question. (I'm dripping with sarcasm as I type this.) Why not name me anything *other* than a name that sounds like a horse owned by a Catholic charity and about to run in the Kentucky Derby?

My cousin, whom I looked up to as a kid, was nicknamed TJ because his name was some obscure family name passed down from generation to generation. I thought the world of TJ and loved that his nickname also just happened to be my initials. So, in one of our moves—it was the move to Arkansas—I decided that not only would my clothes change to fit in with the kids at my school, but my name would change too.

TJ was my new name.

No one would ever know I was Trinity.

I called it my nickname, but it became my identity, as it stuck with me for all of my high school years and into the first part of college.

I had no clue that by telling the world to call me by my initials, I was, in essence, running from who God had created me to be.

There is power in a name.

There is power in our identity.

A Match to End All Matches

Jacob begins to understand this as he sits in the desert.

He's still nervous about meeting his brother, Esau. The man from whom he stole the birthright and blessing is now getting a chance to meet him face-to-face. There's no mother or father to protect Jacob here.

Esau is on his way to meet Jacob, bringing with him four hundred men—this can't be good, can it?

Why isn't he waiting for Jacob to arrive back home?

Is he scared Jacob is coming with an army to take what's rightfully his, now that the birthright and blessing belong to him?

Is he trying to fend off an invasion?

In nervousness and fear Jacob sends his family

ahead of himself in their travels, knowing they would not be attacked without him there.

He sits alone.

Separated from his family.

Separated from his wealth.

Alone.

And God likes to work in the nothing.

Jacob has already taken his first steps by praying to God—trusting God—to help him in this situation. Now is the time for that trust to manifest itself in the biggest experience with God that Jacob and his family have ever experienced.

> And Jacob was left alone.
> —GENESIS 32:24

Suddenly—well, suddenly for us, as the readers of the Genesis story, because the author doesn't give us details as to how quickly this happens—a man, whom theologians and scholars have identified as an angel or messenger of God, starts a wrestling match with Jacob.

In one sense this seems like the most bizarre story to imagine. Alone in the desert, a man, an angel, or a *something* starts an MMA-type fight with Jacob.

Why?

And this isn't just a quick wrestling match that you see at a high school sporting event, either. It's a wrestling match that lasts all night long. We're talking eight to ten hours of continuous fighting here.

And a man wrestled with him until the
breaking of the day.

—GENESIS 32:24

As if that wasn't strange enough for us to wrap our
heads around, the angel-man decides he can't beat
Jacob in this wrestling match, so he touches Jacob's hip
and throws it out of joint:

> When the man saw that he did not prevail
> against Jacob, he touched his hip socket, and
> Jacob's hip was put out of joint as he wrestled
> with him.
>
> —GENESIS 32:25

Now, apparently at this point in the wrestling match,
with fierce pain and adrenaline coursing through him,
Jacob gets the angel-man in some sort of wrestling
hold, and the angel-man cannot break free:

> Then he [the angel-man] said, "Let me go, for
> the day has broken." But Jacob said, "I will not
> let you go unless you bless me."
>
> —GENESIS 32:26

It seems a somewhat odd request from Jacob at first
reading.

But after the contemplation of Jacob's whole life that
we've done, it starts to make sense. Here is Jacob, wrestling with what God has given him for his whole life.

Unhappy with being second.

Not really sure who he is.

Struggling with his identity.

He has finally started to trust God.

Not his stuff.

Not his manipulation.

Not his ability to pull a fast one over anybody to get what he wants.

No hiding or running away.

A man Jacob senses is from God confronts him in the desert, and all Jacob can figure is that if God blesses him, things will be OK.

Maybe Jacob's trust in God is growing faster than we can imagine.

Maybe Jacob has gone all-in with his faith.

It sure appears as if Jacob is pretty adamant—if God blesses him, he will survive whatever is about to come his way when Esau finally shows up on scene.

Then look what happens:

> And he [the angel-man] said to him, "What is your name?"
>
> —GENESIS 32:27

What a question to ask Jacob! Especially because when we first met Jacob, he was trying to be someone else.

He was pretending to be his brother, Esau, remember?

What is your name?

The angel-man might as well have said, "Who are you?"

WHO ARE YOU?

It's a great question for Jacob, but it's also a question for us.

What is your name?

Who are you?

You are made in the image of God.

Not a mistake.

Made with purpose.

Made by the author of the universe.

Made with design, thought through, and executed to perfection.

The almighty God who sees all—all that ever was, all that is, and all that ever will be—has intimate knowledge of you and who He created you to be:

> For you formed my inward parts; you knitted me together in my mother's womb. I praise you, for I am fearfully and wonderfully made. Wonderful are your works; my soul knows it very well. My frame was not hidden from you, when I was being made in secret, intricately woven in the depths of the earth. Your eyes saw my unformed substance; in your book were written, every one of them, the days that

were formed for me, when as yet there were none of them.

—Psalm 139:13–16

David, the author of this psalm, just told us that God intricately wove you together for a purpose. You were designed with a purpose. You were created with a purpose. There are no mistakes. God knew the days you would live the moment He was intricately weaving you together in your mother's womb.

When I was growing up, we found out when I got into school that I had been given the ability to make friends and talk nonstop. It didn't matter whom I was seated next to in class, I could make friends with them and would talk away to them.

I always got in trouble for this. I'm pretty sure I spent the entire third grade year with my desk right next to the teacher's desk. Countless hours were wasted in the principal's office and in meetings with my parents and teachers as they discussed the fact that I could not just shut my mouth.

My daughters both have varying degrees of this ability, which I have passed down to them. We're talkers and socializers. Silence, to us, is something that is meant to be conquered not embraced.

What David's psalm is saying is that God intricately wove me together in my mother's womb knowing all this. He put my physical body together. He saw all the days I would live. He knew the call He would place on my life. He knew where He is going to move me. And in all of that, He threw into the wiring and weaving some extra vocalization and social interaction abilities.

God knew what He was doing.

I am wired and designed the way God intended.

I used to think my humor and social interactive ability were the result of not liking myself very much. I was the skinny kid with big ears that never seemed to fit in. I was always the underdog, never the top dog. I assumed my personality overcompensated for my physical appearance that didn't connect me to the social norms.

What a lie the enemy was trying to sink into my mind!

Or what a lie I was just telling myself.

Based on this way of thinking, I existed as if God made a mistake in my physical formation that I had to subconsciously compensate for in my personality. The kicker is, I took psychology classes and sociology classes in college that basically told me this was the case.

According to our sacred literature, that is nowhere near the case.

My physical form was made with a purpose and plan.

My social abilities were made with a purpose and plan.

My humor was a gift from God, not a subconscious compensation for lack in other areas.

Yes, one area of my life could help develop another, but it was designed that way, not an unforeseen consequence of God's design.

God knew what He was designing and making when He made me.

You already know my childhood wasn't fun to live through. But the reality of my childhood, as I now see it, is that God knew what I would go through. He saw and knew and anticipated it. He knew how it would shape me and affect me and push me and lead me, long before any of those things ever happened.

My childhood was not a shocker to God.

He wasn't caught off guard by my parent's divorce and my ping-pong life. He would use it all, knowing it all from the very beginning, to work out His master plan.

I can be confident in life because I know God is in control.

I can be confident in life because I am not an accident.

I can be confident in life because I have experienced what God knew was coming and because He is working something out that I can't see but He can see.

I can be confident in who He made me to be.

Since I trust God more than I trust myself, the stuff

of this world, or others, I can live in confidence of His words to me.

God took the social abilities I have, coupled with my gift for gab, the experiences of moving all over the globe and always trying to fit in, and made it easy for me to walk into any situation in life now and connect with others. I can be in Paris and people think I'm French. I can be in Miami and I fit right in. I can be in Utah and I make friends.

God knew what He was doing.

The gift of having this ability to be at ease no matter where I find myself is a result of the life I lived and the abilities God gave me.

And you know what?

I would never have been able to plant churches and do missions work without those abilities. God used me to connect with others so they could walk with Him and have the abundant life.

YOU'RE NOT AN ACCIDENT

At the going away party that Elevation Church in Utah threw for my family and me when God was calling us elsewhere to serve, the church arranged for people to stand on stage and share with us how much we meant to them and what we had done in their lives.

It was a little unnerving—like being at your own funeral. They talked about us in the past tense, as if we were never going to be in their lives again.

Several people stood up on the stage to give our eulogies or whatever they were called.

My dearest friend, Andy Casper, was one of the last to get up on stage and say anything. He was short—I mean, he *is* short, but his words were short, as well. He ended it like this: "I always told you, Trinity, that I felt that if I hung out with you enough, I was going to be rich someday. Well, I am. I am rich in my soul more than I have ever been."

The parade of friends telling us how we impacted them made me realize even more that God used everything in our lives to connect us to them, and He would use everything in their lives to connect them to others, and so forth.

God knows what He is doing with us. He has the whole picture in plain sight.

How many times did I doubt God was working during those years? How many times did I doubt my worth?

I have worth because God loves me and has a plan He is working out.

I have no starring role in this grand epic. I am not Matt Damon, but God is using my bit part to impact others and impact eternity.

I have a purpose. I have a plan. I am made the way God wants me to be made and needs me to be made.

You are too.

You are living in this epic.

You are made for this epic. You are crafted exactly how God needs you to be crafted for this epic.

If He needed you to be any different, He would have crafted you that way.

You are not some random accident of genetic collision.

You are purposefully thought out and wonderfully made for the purposes of God.

Paul wrote to the church in Corinth when he was describing who he was as a leader of the early followers of Jesus: "But by the grace of God I am what I am" (1 Cor. 15:10). In other words, Paul is saying, "This is who God made me to be. I am not someone else. I am me!"

No one can be you better than you.

In short, no one *is* you.

No one is designed like you.

God made your personality, knows your quirks, knows the trials you have and will run through, and designed you to be part of His grand epic.

And you can only be part of this grand epic by playing the part of *you*.

Not only are you made in God's image, with worth and value inherent in your very essence, but when you trust in God and follow after His Son, Jesus, you also have a new identity in Christ.

This is what our sacred Scripture tells those of us who follow after Jesus: We are *new* in Christ. We are not the same. Our identity is not in our old defense mechanisms and searches for freedom. Our identity is in Christ.

Do you get that?

Your identity is not in you alone.

Your identity is in Christ.

You don't ever have to worry about being good enough or smart enough or pretty enough to achieve some perfect goal. All that matters is that Christ is perfect enough and that your identity is in Him.

You don't need a man to gain security in this world; you need *the* Man!

You don't need to achieve professional success in your work; you're successful because *He's* successful!

It doesn't matter what others think, what they do, or what they get. You can walk with confidence, your head held high, knowing that in Christ you are perfect because He is perfect. You are free because He is free.

The more you ground yourself in this truth of being in Christ, the easier it will be to keep yourself from falling into insecure behaviors, defense mechanisms, or hatred of who you are.

Paul told the followers of Jesus who lived in Ephesus this:

> Assuming that you have heard about him and were taught in him, as the truth is in Jesus, to put off your old self, which belongs to your

former manner of life and is corrupt through deceitful desires, and to be renewed in the spirit of your minds, and to put on the new self, created after the likeness of God in true righteousness and holiness.

—Ephesians 4:21–24

Put off the ideas and mind-set you had before you decided to trust in Jesus.

Put off the want of what others have.

Put off the want of making it to the top of some invisible social pyramid.

Put off the want of being admired by the world.

Put off the want of building your own memorials.

This new life of trust means a renewing of who we are.

We are in Christ!

We are not captives to our old mind-set.

We can walk in freedom.

What is your name?

You can answer that with confidence, knowing that Christ is putting His seal of approval on you: "I am _____."

BEING WHO WE ARE

And he [the angel-man] said to him, "What is your name?" And he said, "Jacob."

—Genesis 32:27

The first time we were introduced to Jacob, he was asked who he was, and he professed to be his brother. Now, Jacob is asked again who he is, and he doesn't hesitate in the least to declare that he is Jacob.

No more pretending.

No more trickery.

Jacob is finally comfortable in his own skin.

What a feeling of freedom!

Contentment and security in one's self.

And the great thing is, now that Jacob is comfortable being Jacob, God can use him the way He had used his grandfather, Abraham, and his father, Isaac.

> Then he [the angel-man] said, "Your name shall no longer be called Jacob, but Israel, for you have striven with God and with men, and have prevailed."
>
> —GENESIS 32:28

Maybe this struggle with God and men that the angel-man talks about is Jacob struggling to come to grips with being Jacob. Maybe the struggle is coming to grips with the way God made him to be and who he is.

Maybe that is part of the designed journey for you and me—this struggle to find security in who we are.

Jacob has come to grips with the fact that he is not Esau.

He is Jacob.

God could not use Jacob the way He intended to use Jacob when Jacob was wishing he were someone else. Now he is Israel! Not only does history from this point on start recording the fathers of Judaism as Abraham, Isaac, and Jacob, but also a great nation is named after Jacob's new name!

How can God use you and me when we're wishing we were someone else?

When I began to trust in Christ, my mind-set started to change. This was most obvious when it came to my name. The initials were ditched, and I embraced my birth name. *Trinity.*

No longer did I introduce myself as T. J. Jordan. I was Trinity Jordan.

I wasn't worried about what others thought. It is a very religious-sounding name, true, and my parents were not even heavily religious people. My dad saw an Italian spaghetti western movie where the cowboy was named Trinity, and I happened to be the benefactor of this movie-watching experience.

Now I was OK with this.

It's my story. God knew it was going to happen. He wasn't shocked when my dad suggested the name to my mother and she agreed.

Now, when God asks who I am, I can reply with confidence with my birth-given name, knowing that in Christ I am worthy, valued, and approved. I am not initials from a boyhood family admiration.

And you know what?

It was this first act, these first steps of confidence in my identity in Christ, that allowed me to start walking in a way that the fruit of God could start to cultivate itself in my life in immeasurable ways.

I am not my cousin.

I am not my father.

I am not my grandfather.

I am not my brother.

I am not my coworker.

I am not that other pastor from that other church.

I am in Christ.

Also:

You are not someone else.

You are not your parents.

You are not your siblings.

You are not your friends.

You are in Christ.

What is your name?

In Exodus 20 we find a list of the Ten Commandments that were given to Moses by God. The first nine commandments are externally observable actions. You can see when someone breaks the first commandment and goes off to worship another god. You can see when someone breaks the second commandment and carves an image to bow down to. You can hear someone break the third commandment and take the name of God in vain.

And so on. The first nine commands are observable. They happen right in front of our eyes.

The tenth commandment is different, though.

The first nine commandments are one sentence, tight and sweet. The tenth commandment takes up the largest amount of space. More words, more details.

But that is not all.

It says:

> You shall not covet your neighbor's house; you shall not covet your neighbor's wife, or his male servant, or his female servant, or his ox, or his donkey, or anything that is your neighbor's.
>
> —EXODUS 20:17

Coveting.

It's not very observable.

I can't observe you coveting the life someone else is living.

I can't see the person walking down the street coveting the shirt I'm wearing.

I can't see you wanting something else than what you have.

I can't see you desiring to be someone else.

The reason this command is so different from the other nine commandments is this: if you trust God and follow the first nine commandments, then you will find contentment and not want the life of anyone else. You will be happy with the life you were given and the things you were given, and you will be secure in what you have.

Maybe God was telling Moses that the first nine commandments were ways they were meant to walk with God and the tenth wasn't so much a commandment as what would happen in your life if you were already following and trusting God.

If you do these nine things, then this tenth thing will happen in your life.

Maybe that's why the tenth commandment is so different. Maybe it really isn't a commandment like we think it is.

No More Sabotage

> So Jacob called the name of the place Peniel, saying, "For I have seen God face to face, and yet my life has been delivered." The sun rose upon him as he passed Penuel, limping because of his hip.
>
> —Genesis 32:30–31

Jacob builds another memorial. This time, though, there are slight differences in his memorial-building experience than the first time around. Some scholars and teachers claim this isn't a memorial he builds at all, in fact, but an altar to worship God.

What I can tell you is that the place is named not for Jacob, but for God. *Peniel* means "face of God," not "I saw the face of God." What has always been about Jacob is now about God. Just look at the picture the text paints here: Jacob, in his humility and humanity, is limping away from a place he names the "face of God."

He was not in control.

He knew who God was—and it wasn't him.

He worshipped God for the rest of his life.

You can either build memorials to yourself, living in the cycle of defense mechanisms, and sabotaged living, or you can build memorials to God and worship Him.

If you could pick to win, why would you ever pick to lose?

If you could pick to worship what is real, why would you ever pick to worship what is temporary?

Worshipping, submitting, and adoring something other than yourself will lead you to confidence in your identity.

Do not let your insecurity sabotage your identity.

Living in Christ is the only answer to subverting the natural human tendencies that are our insecurities.

Again, imitating others will not free you. Your desires will never bring you freedom. Only Christ can free you from the lack of security that haunts your very identity.

My prayer for you is that you will put your trust in Him.

That you will sweat and strain as you row your kayak out to mile-marker one in the middle of the ocean.

That you will strain to collect the one-gallon bucket of seawater.

That you will row back to shore tired and fatigued.

That you will spend hours milking cows, churning milk, and drying out seawater.

And that when all the hard work is done...

When you pass right by all the chances to return to who you used to be...

When you put on a different mind-set...

And take a bite of that butter...

That you would experience freedom.

Freedom like you've never tasted before.

And that the sabotage would finally end.

NOTES

CHAPTER 1
THE SABOTAGE BEGINS

1. John Steinbeck, *The Winter of Our Discontent* (New York: Penguin Classics, 2008), 44.
2. Katie Kindelan, "Cal Ripken Jr. Seeks Help in Finding Mom's Abductor," August 3, 2012, ABC News, http://abcnews.go.com/blogs/headlines/2012/08/cal-ripken-jr-seeks-help-in-finding-moms-abducter/ (accessed November 15, 2012).
3. F. L. Gross, *Introducing Erik Erikson,* (Lanham, MD: University Press of America, 1987).

CHAPTER 2
MEMORIAL OF PRIDE

1. As quoted in "Death of a Genius," *LIFE*, May 2, 1955.

CHAPTER 3
WHAT IS THAT TO YOU?

1. Mike Krzyzewski with Donald T. Phillips, *Leading With the Heart* (New York: Warner Books, Inc., 2000), 54.

CHAPTER 4
FEAR OF FAIR

1. Rick Warren, August 1, 2012 (6:20 p.m.) post on Twitter, https://twitter.com/RickWarren/status/230805243384963072 (accessed November 20, 2012).
2. ChoSunMedia.com, "Korea Plagued by Controversial Rulings at London Games," August 1, 2012, http://english.chosun.com/site/data/html_dir/2012/08/01/2012080101451.html (accessed January 25, 2013).

CHAPTER 5
NO ADDITIVES ALLOWED

1. Mark Hyman, "Finger Lickin' Good," May 16, 2012,
http://drhyman.com/blog/2012/05/16/finger-lickin-good/
(accessed November 21, 2012).

CHAPTER 6
LIFE WITH THE LIFE-GIVER

1. Oswald Chambers, "Where the Battle Is Won or Lost,"
My Utmost for His Highest (Grand Rapids, MI: Discovery
House Publishers, 1992).

CHAPTER 7
THE LIFE YOU ALWAYS WANTED

1. William P. Young, *The Shack* (Newbury Park, CA: Wind-
blown Media, 2007).

CHAPTER 8
WHAT IS YOUR NAME?

1. Thinkexist.com, "Judy Garland Quotes," http://thinkexist
.com/quotation/always_be_a_first-rate_version_of_
yourself/210051.html (accessed November 28, 2012).
2. Cyrus Diaz, "Identity," http://www.poemhunter.com/
poem/identity-54/ (accessed November 28, 2012). Permission requested.

FREE NEWSLETTERS
TO HELP EMPOWER YOUR LIFE

Why subscribe today?

☐ **DELIVERED DIRECTLY TO YOU.** All you have to do is open your inbox and read.

☐ **EXCLUSIVE CONTENT.** We cover the news overlooked by the mainstream press.

☐ **STAY CURRENT.** Find the latest court rulings, revivals, and cultural trends.

☐ **UPDATE OTHERS.** Easy to forward to friends and family with the click of your mouse.

CHOOSE THE E-NEWSLETTER THAT INTERESTS YOU MOST:

- Christian news
- Daily devotionals
- Spiritual empowerment
- And much, much more

SIGN UP AT: **http://freenewsletters.charismamag.com**

8178